Nature Positive Economy: Sustainability, Ecosystem Restoration, and Biodiversity Conservation

Copyright

Published by Global Climate Solutions

ISBN: 978-1-991369-00-0 (eBook)

ISBN: 978-1-991369-01-7 (Paperback)

ISBN: 978-1-991369-02-4 (Hardcopy)

Preface

The world faces an urgent need to transition to an economic model that prioritizes sustainability, ecosystem restoration, and biodiversity conservation. The *Nature Positive Economy* (NPE) offers a transformative framework that integrates nature into economic decision-making, ensuring that businesses, governments, and communities align their activities with ecological well-being.

This book explores the core principles, strategies, and policies necessary for achieving a nature-positive economy. It examines how industries can adopt sustainable practices, how economic incentives can drive nature recovery, and how collaboration across sectors can support biodiversity and climate resilience. With a growing recognition that environmental sustainability is fundamental to long-term prosperity, this book provides practical solutions for integrating nature into economic systems.

By drawing upon international frameworks, innovative policies, and emerging trends, *Nature Positive Economy* serves as a guide for policymakers, business leaders, sustainability professionals, and researchers. It is my hope that this book will inspire action toward creating an economy where nature is not just protected, but actively regenerated for the benefit of future generations.

Robert C. Brears

Table of Contents

Introduction

The "Introduction" chapter sets the stage for understanding the concept of a Nature Positive Economy (NPE). It explores the foundational principles and the urgent need for a shift toward sustainable economic practices that prioritize ecosystem health and biodiversity. This chapter introduces the framework of the NPE, outlining its core strategies and the role it plays in addressing global environmental challenges such as climate change and biodiversity loss. It also highlights the benefits of adopting a nature-positive approach, not only for the environment but for long-term economic resilience and human wellbeing.

What is the Nature Positive Economy?

The NPE is an innovative framework that integrates environmental sustainability into the heart of economic development, aiming to restore and protect natural ecosystems while promoting human wellbeing and prosperity.

Definition of Nature Positive Economy

The NPE is an economic model that places environmental health and human wellbeing at the center of economic decision-making and development. It prioritizes the protection, restoration, and sustainable use of natural resources, ensuring that economic activities contribute to preserving biodiversity and maintaining the planet's ecological balance. The NPE seeks to integrate nature into the economy by recognizing the value of ecosystems and the services they provide, such as clean air, water, carbon storage, and pollination.

This model emphasizes halting and reversing biodiversity loss, supporting industries in adopting sustainable practices, and creating economic opportunities through nature recovery efforts. It encourages investments in green jobs, renewable energy, and nature-based solutions that simultaneously address environmental and social challenges. By fostering collaboration between governments, businesses, and communities, the NPE aims to align economic growth with ecological sustainability.

At its core, the NPE challenges traditional economic models that prioritize short-term profits over long-term environmental and societal benefits. Instead, it promotes a vision where nature and the economy work in harmony, ensuring that natural ecosystems are conserved, restored, and leveraged responsibly to achieve sustainable development for current and future generations.

Core principles: environmental health and human wellbeing.

The core principles of a NPE revolve around achieving a balance between environmental health and human wellbeing, recognizing their interdependence.

Environmental Health:

- Protecting and restoring ecosystems is fundamental to maintaining biodiversity and the ecological processes that sustain life.
- Prioritizing actions to halt and reverse environmental degradation, including deforestation, pollution, and habitat destruction, ensures long-term planetary health.
- Sustainable resource management focuses on reducing waste, promoting circular economies, and limiting the overexploitation of natural assets.

Human Wellbeing:

- A NPE emphasizes equitable access to the benefits of healthy ecosystems, such as clean water, air, food security, and protection from climate-related risks.
- It fosters the creation of green jobs and livelihoods, enabling individuals and communities to thrive while contributing to environmental stewardship.

- Addressing social equity, particularly for vulnerable populations, ensures inclusive development where everyone benefits from nature-positive solutions.

Together, these principles guide an economic transition toward a future that prioritizes both planetary resilience and human prosperity.

Historical context and evolution of the concept

The concept of a NPE emerged in response to growing concerns over the unsustainable exploitation of natural resources and its impact on biodiversity, climate stability, and human wellbeing. The term gained prominence in the late 2010s, catalyzed by global environmental movements and international agreements such as the Convention on Biological Diversity (CBD) and the Sustainable Development Goals (SDGs).

The Kunming-Montreal Global Biodiversity Framework, adopted in 2022, set ambitious targets to halt biodiversity loss and restore ecosystems, encouraging the integration of nature into economic systems. Simultaneously, businesses and governments began acknowledging the economic risks associated with environmental degradation, such as supply chain disruptions and loss of ecosystem services.

The NPE evolved from traditional conservation models by emphasizing economic opportunities in nature recovery, such as green jobs and sustainable industries. Today, it represents a forward-looking vision where economic growth is harmonized with environmental stewardship, addressing both global challenges and local needs.

Why Do We Need an NPE?

We need a NPE to address the urgent challenges of biodiversity loss, environmental degradation, and climate change while fostering sustainable economic growth and improving human wellbeing.

Current environmental and economic challenges

The world faces mounting environmental and economic challenges that threaten the stability of ecosystems, societies, and economies. Climate change, driven by greenhouse gas emissions, has led to rising global temperatures, extreme weather events, and shifts in ecosystems, impacting agriculture, water resources, and livelihoods. Concurrently, biodiversity loss is accelerating at an alarming rate due to habitat destruction, pollution, overexploitation of natural resources, and invasive species. These trends undermine the ecological balance that supports food security, clean water, and air quality, which are essential for human survival.

On the economic front, unsustainable practices have resulted in resource depletion, disrupted supply chains, and escalating costs from environmental degradation. For instance, deforestation and soil erosion reduce agricultural productivity, while water scarcity threatens industries and communities worldwide. Developing countries, often most reliant on natural resources, face significant challenges as environmental damage exacerbates poverty and inequality.

The convergence of these environmental and economic crises necessitates a shift in how economies operate. Traditional growth models, which prioritize short-term gains over long-term sustainability, are no longer viable. Addressing these interconnected challenges requires a NPE that prioritizes the restoration of ecosystems, sustainable resource management, and equitable economic opportunities to ensure resilience and prosperity for future generations.

Potential benefits of NPE

A NPE offers numerous benefits by aligning economic activities with environmental restoration and human wellbeing. One of its primary advantages is the ability to halt and reverse biodiversity loss, safeguarding ecosystems that provide essential services such as clean water, pollination, and carbon storage. Healthy ecosystems enhance climate resilience, reducing the impacts of extreme weather events, floods, and droughts on communities and economies.

From an economic perspective, the NPE fosters sustainable growth by creating green jobs in sectors like renewable energy, conservation, and sustainable agriculture. These jobs not only drive innovation and productivity but also provide stable livelihoods, particularly in vulnerable regions. By promoting circular economies and sustainable resource use, an NPE reduces waste and dependence on finite resources, enhancing long-term economic stability.

Socially, the NPE supports equitable development by ensuring that communities benefit from restored ecosystems and sustainable practices. It provides opportunities for indigenous and local communities to lead conservation efforts while improving their quality of life.

Moreover, the NPE addresses global challenges like climate change and food insecurity, contributing to healthier, more sustainable societies. By investing in nature, economies not only protect the planet but also unlock pathways to a more resilient and prosperous future for all.

Urgency for action

The urgency for action toward a NPE stems from the accelerating degradation of ecosystems, biodiversity loss, and climate change. Scientists warn that many natural systems are approaching irreversible tipping points, threatening food security, water availability, and global stability. Traditional economic models continue to drive unsustainable resource use, exacerbating these crises. Delaying action risks further ecological collapse, economic instability, and social inequality. Transitioning to an NPE offers a crucial opportunity to restore balance, mitigate climate impacts, and secure a sustainable future. Immediate, coordinated efforts are essential to ensure resilience for both the planet and future generations.

How This Book Will Guide You

This book serves as a practical guide to understanding the principles of a NPE and implementing strategies that align economic growth with environmental restoration and human wellbeing.

Purpose of the book

The purpose of this book is to provide a comprehensive understanding of the NPE and its transformative potential to address pressing global challenges. As the world faces unprecedented environmental degradation, biodiversity loss, and social inequalities, a new economic framework is essential to ensure a sustainable and equitable future. This book aims to bridge the gap between theory and practice, offering insights into how economies can shift from exploiting natural resources to restoring and valuing them.

The book is designed to serve as a practical resource for policymakers, business leaders, sustainability professionals, and communities seeking to adopt nature-positive strategies. By exploring the principles, challenges, and opportunities of the NPE, it equips readers with the knowledge and tools to take actionable steps toward a more sustainable economy. It highlights pathways for protecting and restoring ecosystems, fostering green jobs, supporting industries in adopting sustainable practices, and enabling equitable development for all.

Ultimately, this book aspires to inspire a shared vision where economic growth harmonizes with ecological restoration and human wellbeing. It provides a roadmap for transitioning to an economy that not only preserves the planet's natural capital but also creates lasting prosperity for current and future generations.

Overview of chapters

This book is structured to guide readers through the principles, challenges, and opportunities of a NPE, offering actionable insights at every stage.

The Introduction establishes the foundation of the NPE, explaining its core concepts and the urgent need for a new economic model that prioritizes environmental health and human wellbeing. It sets the stage for the detailed exploration of key themes in subsequent chapters.

Chapter 1: Protecting and Restoring Natural Areas delves into the critical role of natural ecosystems in sustaining biodiversity, climate regulation, and human wellbeing. It outlines strategies for protecting these areas and scaling up restoration efforts.

Chapter 2: Halting and Reversing Biodiversity Loss examines the causes and consequences of biodiversity decline, exploring frameworks, policies, and technological innovations to reverse these trends.

Chapter 3: Creating Jobs in Nature Recovery highlights the economic potential of green jobs and the industries driving employment in conservation, renewable energy, and sustainable tourism.

Chapter 4: Helping Industries Adopt Sustainable Practices focuses on transitioning businesses to sustainable models, showcasing tools, incentives, and successful examples.

Chapter 5: Conserving and Restoring Ecosystem Benefits explores strategies to protect ecosystem services like water security and carbon storage, including innovative financing mechanisms.

The Conclusion synthesizes the book's insights, providing a call to action for embracing an NPE.

Target audience and intended outcomes

The target audience for this book includes policymakers, business leaders, sustainability professionals, academics, and community advocates seeking practical solutions to environmental and economic challenges. It is also intended for individuals passionate about promoting biodiversity, climate resilience, and equitable development.

The book aims to equip readers with a clear understanding of the NPE and actionable strategies to integrate its principles into decision-making and operations. By highlighting opportunities for green growth, sustainable practices, and community empowerment, the book seeks to inspire transformative change, enabling readers to contribute to a future where economic prosperity aligns with ecological and social wellbeing.

Chapter 1: Protecting and Restoring Natural Areas

Natural areas are the foundation of life on Earth, providing essential services such as clean air, water, climate regulation, and biodiversity. Yet, these ecosystems are under immense pressure from deforestation, habitat destruction, and unsustainable resource use, leading to widespread degradation and biodiversity loss. Protecting and restoring natural areas is critical not only for the health of the planet but also for human survival and economic stability.

This chapter explores the vital role natural areas play in maintaining ecological balance and supporting human wellbeing. It delves into strategies for safeguarding these environments, from establishing protected areas to leveraging indigenous knowledge and rewilding efforts. The chapter also examines the challenges and opportunities in scaling up restoration initiatives, including funding constraints, urbanization, and the need for collaborative solutions. By highlighting the importance of integrating modern technology with traditional practices, this chapter provides a comprehensive roadmap for preserving and restoring natural ecosystems as a cornerstone of the NPE.

The Role of Natural Areas in the Economy

Natural areas play a crucial role in the economy by providing ecosystem services that support agriculture, industry, climate regulation, and human wellbeing, forming the backbone of sustainable development.

Importance of natural areas for biodiversity

Natural areas are vital for maintaining biodiversity, which underpins the health and resilience of ecosystems worldwide. These areas serve as habitats for a vast array of plant, animal, and microbial species, many of which are interdependent and essential for ecological balance. Biodiversity within natural areas contributes to critical processes such as pollination, nutrient cycling, water purification, and climate regulation. Without these natural systems, ecosystems would lose their ability to function effectively, jeopardizing both environmental health and human survival.

Natural areas act as genetic reservoirs, preserving species diversity that supports agricultural productivity and resilience. For example, wild plant species found in forests and grasslands often carry traits that can improve crop resistance to pests, diseases, and climate change. Additionally, biodiversity in natural areas provides the foundation for pharmaceutical discoveries, with many medicines derived from compounds found in plants and microorganisms.

The loss of biodiversity in natural areas can trigger cascading effects, leading to ecosystem collapse and reduced capacity to provide essential services. Protecting and restoring these areas is crucial for halting biodiversity loss, ensuring ecological stability, and mitigating the impacts of climate change.

Investing in the conservation of natural areas not only preserves biodiversity but also safeguards the economic and social benefits they provide, ensuring a sustainable future for all.

Contribution to climate regulation

Natural areas play a critical role in climate regulation by acting as carbon sinks, stabilizing temperatures, and mitigating the impacts of climate change. Forests, wetlands, grasslands, and oceans absorb and store vast amounts of carbon dioxide, reducing greenhouse gas concentrations in the atmosphere. For instance, tropical rainforests like the Amazon act as "lungs of the Earth," sequestering billions of tons of carbon annually. Similarly, coastal ecosystems such as mangroves, seagrasses, and salt marshes store carbon more efficiently than many terrestrial ecosystems, offering a natural solution to combat climate change.

In addition to carbon sequestration, natural areas regulate local and regional climates by influencing temperature, humidity, and precipitation patterns. Forests provide shade and release moisture through transpiration, cooling the atmosphere and creating conditions that sustain rainfall. Grasslands and wetlands help manage water cycles, reducing the risk of droughts and floods. These climate-regulating functions are essential for maintaining stable environments that support agriculture, industry, and human livelihoods.

However, the destruction of natural areas significantly undermines these benefits. Deforestation, land degradation, and wetland loss release stored carbon back into the atmosphere, exacerbating climate change. Preserving and restoring these ecosystems not only strengthens their capacity to regulate the climate but also enhances their resilience against extreme weather events, ensuring long-term sustainability and stability for both natural and human systems.

Benefits to human wellbeing and local economies

Natural areas are indispensable for human wellbeing and local economies, providing essential services that sustain life and support economic activity. These ecosystems offer a range of benefits, including clean air, fresh water, food security, and protection from natural disasters, all of which are critical for healthy, thriving communities.

Human Wellbeing

Natural areas directly contribute to physical and mental health. Forests, wetlands, and urban green spaces improve air quality by filtering pollutants, while healthy watersheds supply clean drinking water to millions. Access to natural spaces has been shown to reduce stress, improve mental health, and enhance overall quality of life. Additionally, these areas provide resources for food and medicine, with many rural communities depending on forests and rivers for their sustenance and livelihoods.

Biodiverse ecosystems also play a protective role, acting as natural barriers against extreme weather events. Mangroves and coral reefs, for example, reduce the impact of coastal storms and prevent erosion, safeguarding homes and infrastructure. Wetlands and forests mitigate the risk of flooding by absorbing excess water, providing a buffer for vulnerable communities during heavy rainfall.

Local Economies

Natural areas are a cornerstone of local economies, particularly in regions reliant on agriculture, tourism, and natural resource-based industries. Ecotourism, for instance, generates significant income and creates jobs in conservation, guiding, and hospitality. Protected areas and national parks attract millions of visitors annually, contributing to local development and raising awareness of environmental preservation.

Sustainable management of natural resources supports long-term economic growth. Fisheries, forestry, and agriculture all benefit from the biodiversity and ecological balance maintained by healthy ecosystems. Additionally, ecosystem services such as pollination, soil fertility, and water filtration are invaluable to these industries, ensuring productivity and reducing operational costs.

By protecting and restoring natural areas, we not only secure these vital benefits but also build resilient communities and economies that thrive in harmony with nature. Investing in the preservation of ecosystems is an investment in human wellbeing and sustainable economic prosperity.

Key Strategies for Protection

Key strategies for protecting natural areas focus on preserving biodiversity, maintaining ecosystem services, and ensuring sustainable use through policies, community involvement, and innovative approaches.

Protected areas and wildlife corridors

Protected areas and wildlife corridors are essential strategies for preserving biodiversity, maintaining ecological integrity, and ensuring the survival of countless species. Protected areas, such as national parks, nature reserves, and marine sanctuaries, are designated regions where human activities are limited or prohibited to conserve ecosystems and their biodiversity. These areas serve as safe havens for plants and animals, protecting them from threats like habitat destruction, pollution, and overexploitation.

Protected areas are critical for maintaining ecological balance. They safeguard habitats that support key ecosystem services such as carbon sequestration, water filtration, and soil fertility. By preserving these ecosystems, protected areas also contribute to human wellbeing, supporting sustainable livelihoods through ecotourism, research, and education. Globally, initiatives like the Kunming-Montreal Global Biodiversity Framework aim to expand protected areas, targeting 30% of the planet's land and oceans under protection by 2030.

Wildlife corridors complement protected areas by connecting fragmented habitats, allowing species to move freely between regions. These corridors are especially important for migratory species and animals with large home ranges, such as elephants and big cats. By facilitating movement, corridors help maintain genetic diversity, reduce inbreeding, and ensure the long-term survival of populations.

Corridors also mitigate the effects of habitat fragmentation caused by urbanization, agriculture, and infrastructure development. For example, overpasses and underpasses for wildlife on roads and highways reduce vehicle collisions while maintaining connectivity between habitats. Similarly, riparian corridors along rivers support aquatic and terrestrial species by providing continuous habitats.

Implementing and managing protected areas and wildlife corridors requires collaboration among governments, local communities, and conservation organizations. Local involvement is crucial for the success of these efforts, as it fosters stewardship and aligns conservation goals with community needs. Financial support, effective enforcement, and monitoring are also vital to ensure these areas fulfill their ecological functions.

By combining protected areas with well-designed wildlife corridors, we can create resilient landscapes that support biodiversity, ecosystem services, and human livelihoods. Together, these strategies are fundamental for a NPE, ensuring the coexistence of thriving ecosystems and sustainable development.

Indigenous Leadership and Knowledge

Indigenous leadership and traditional knowledge are essential components of effective conservation and restoration strategies. Indigenous peoples have lived in close connection with their environments for generations, developing deep ecological understanding and sustainable practices that protect biodiversity and support ecosystem health. Recognizing and integrating their leadership and knowledge into conservation efforts is critical for achieving long-term environmental and social goals.

The Value of Indigenous Knowledge

Indigenous communities possess a wealth of knowledge about local ecosystems, including plant and animal behavior, seasonal changes, and sustainable resource use. This understanding, rooted in lived experience and cultural traditions, often surpasses scientific knowledge in specific contexts. For example, indigenous fire management practices in Australia, known as "cultural burning," have proven highly effective in reducing wildfire risks while promoting biodiversity. Similarly, indigenous agroforestry systems combine ecological balance with food production, offering sustainable alternatives to industrial agriculture.

Indigenous knowledge is not only practical but also holistic. It incorporates spiritual and cultural dimensions, fostering a deep respect for nature and emphasizing the interconnectedness of all life. This perspective aligns closely with the principles of a NPE, which seeks to harmonize human activities with ecological systems.

Indigenous Leadership in Conservation

Indigenous peoples play a leading role in conserving and managing natural areas worldwide. While they comprise less than 5% of the global population, they steward more than a quarter of the Earth's land surface, including some of the most biodiverse regions. Their leadership has been instrumental in the establishment and management of protected areas, community conservancies, and sustainable development initiatives.

Programs that empower indigenous communities to lead conservation efforts often yield significant environmental and social benefits. For instance, community-managed forests in the Amazon have shown lower deforestation rates compared to other areas, thanks to indigenous oversight. In Canada, indigenous-led marine conservation initiatives have protected critical coastal habitats while supporting local livelihoods through ecotourism and sustainable fisheries.

Collaboration and Respect

Successful integration of indigenous leadership and knowledge into conservation requires genuine collaboration and respect for their rights and autonomy. Governments, organizations, and stakeholders must engage with indigenous communities as equal partners, ensuring their voices are heard and their contributions valued. Legal recognition of indigenous land rights is crucial for enabling effective stewardship and protecting their cultural heritage.

Additionally, blending indigenous knowledge with scientific research can enhance conservation outcomes. For example, co-management models that combine traditional practices with modern technology offer innovative solutions to complex environmental challenges.

Indigenous leadership and knowledge are indispensable for a NPE. By empowering indigenous communities and respecting their contributions, we can protect biodiversity, restore ecosystems, and promote sustainable development. This approach not only ensures environmental resilience but also upholds social justice and cultural diversity, creating a better future for both people and the planet.

Rewilding and Nature Restoration Projects

Rewilding and nature restoration projects are transformative approaches to rebuilding ecosystems, enhancing biodiversity, and addressing the impacts of climate change. By allowing natural processes to recover and flourish, these projects create self-sustaining landscapes that require minimal human intervention, fostering resilience and restoring balance to degraded environments.

The Concept of Rewilding

Rewilding involves reintroducing native species, restoring ecological processes, and removing barriers that hinder the natural dynamics of ecosystems. This approach goes beyond traditional conservation by focusing on the restoration of wilderness and ecological functions rather than simply protecting existing habitats. Key goals of rewilding include increasing biodiversity, improving ecosystem services, and mitigating climate change impacts.

For example, the reintroduction of keystone species such as wolves in Yellowstone National Park led to trophic cascades that transformed the park's ecosystem. By controlling deer populations, wolves allowed vegetation to regenerate, stabilizing riverbanks and improving water quality. This demonstrates how rewilding can restore natural balance and create thriving ecosystems.

Nature Restoration Projects

Nature restoration projects aim to repair degraded ecosystems and recover their ability to provide essential services. These projects often involve active interventions, such as replanting native vegetation, restoring wetlands, and removing invasive species. They are particularly critical in areas heavily impacted by human activities, such as deforested landscapes, polluted waterways, and urban areas.

One notable example is the restoration of peatlands, which serve as vital carbon sinks and habitats for unique species. Restoring degraded peatlands prevents further carbon emissions, enhances water regulation, and supports biodiversity. Similarly, coastal restoration projects, such as mangrove reforestation, protect communities from storm surges while providing critical habitats for marine life.

Benefits of Rewilding and Restoration

Both rewilding and restoration projects offer numerous environmental, social, and economic benefits. They enhance biodiversity by creating habitats for plants and animals, improve ecosystem services like water purification and carbon storage, and increase climate resilience. Additionally, these projects often generate economic opportunities, such as ecotourism and green jobs in habitat management and monitoring.

Restoration projects also benefit human communities by improving air and water quality, reducing flood risks, and offering recreational spaces that promote wellbeing. By reconnecting people with nature, these efforts foster a deeper appreciation for the environment and encourage sustainable practices.

Challenges and Collaboration

Despite their benefits, rewilding and restoration projects face challenges, including land-use conflicts, funding constraints, and public resistance to changes in landscape management. Collaboration among governments, conservation organizations, and local communities is essential to address these challenges and ensure project success. Public education and community involvement are key to building support and achieving long-term goals.

Rewilding and nature restoration are powerful tools for creating a NPE. By revitalizing degraded ecosystems and enabling natural processes to thrive, these initiatives contribute to biodiversity conservation, climate mitigation, and sustainable development, paving the way for a healthier planet and prosperous future.

Challenges and Opportunities

Addressing the challenges and seizing the opportunities in protecting and restoring natural areas are essential for achieving long-term biodiversity conservation and sustainable development goals.

Urbanization and Land-Use Conflicts

Urbanization and land-use conflicts pose significant challenges to the conservation and restoration of natural areas. As cities expand to accommodate growing populations, forests, wetlands, and other natural habitats are often cleared to make way for housing, infrastructure, and agriculture. This encroachment not only leads to habitat destruction but also fragments ecosystems, disrupting the migration patterns and lifecycles of wildlife.

Urbanization often prioritizes short-term economic gains over long-term ecological sustainability. For example, the conversion of wetlands into urban developments may provide immediate housing solutions but compromises critical ecosystem services such as flood regulation, water purification, and biodiversity support. Similarly, agricultural expansion into forested areas can lead to deforestation and soil degradation, further exacerbating climate change and reducing land productivity over time.

Land-use conflicts arise when competing interests—such as agriculture, industry, urban development, and conservation—vie for the same resources. These conflicts are particularly acute in regions where economic development is prioritized without regard for environmental consequences. For instance, infrastructure projects like highways or mining operations often lead to irreversible damage to natural areas, sparking tensions between developers, conservationists, and local communities.

Addressing these challenges requires integrated land-use planning that balances economic growth with ecological preservation. Tools such as zoning laws, environmental impact assessments, and green infrastructure can help minimize conflicts. Additionally, promoting urban green spaces and sustainable land-use practices can enhance biodiversity within urban areas while reducing pressure on surrounding natural habitats. Collaborative approaches involving governments, businesses, and communities are essential to reconcile development needs with environmental protection, ensuring a sustainable coexistence of human and natural systems.

Urbanization and land-use conflicts highlight the urgent need for thoughtful policies and innovative solutions to protect natural areas. By managing land resources responsibly, we can support both urban development and biodiversity conservation, paving the way for a balanced and sustainable future.

Securing Funding for Large-Scale Restoration

Funding is a critical challenge for large-scale restoration projects, which require substantial financial resources for planning, implementation, and long-term maintenance. Despite the clear ecological and economic benefits of restoration, securing adequate and consistent funding remains a significant barrier, particularly in regions with limited financial capacity or competing development priorities.

Traditional funding sources, such as government budgets and philanthropic donations, often fall short of meeting the financial needs of large-scale restoration efforts. Many governments face competing demands for limited resources, which can lead to underinvestment in environmental initiatives. Similarly, reliance on charitable contributions can be inconsistent, making it difficult to sustain long-term projects.

Innovative financing mechanisms are increasingly being explored to address these funding gaps. For example, carbon credits offer a market-based approach where businesses and governments invest in restoration projects to offset their carbon emissions. Similarly, debt-for-nature swaps allow countries to reduce their debt in exchange for commitments to protect and restore ecosystems. These mechanisms not only provide funding but also incentivize sustainable practices and international cooperation.

Public-private partnerships are another effective model for securing funding. By leveraging private sector investments alongside public resources, these collaborations can mobilize significant capital while aligning restoration goals with business interests. Examples include corporate sponsorships of reforestation projects or sustainable agriculture initiatives that benefit both companies and local communities.

To ensure long-term financial sustainability, restoration projects must also generate tangible economic benefits. Initiatives such as ecotourism, sustainable forestry, and renewable energy projects within restored areas can create revenue streams that support ongoing management and maintenance.

Securing funding for large-scale restoration requires a multifaceted approach that combines traditional and innovative financing solutions. By prioritizing investment in restoration, governments, businesses, and communities can unlock the ecological and economic benefits of healthy, resilient ecosystems.

Collaborations Between Public, Private, and Community Stakeholders

Effective collaborations between public, private, and community stakeholders are essential for the success of large-scale conservation and restoration initiatives. Each group brings unique resources, expertise, and perspectives, making partnerships a powerful tool for addressing complex environmental challenges.

Public Sector Contributions

Governments play a central role by providing policy frameworks, funding, and enforcement mechanisms. Public agencies can designate protected areas, enact environmental regulations, and allocate resources for restoration efforts. Additionally, governments can incentivize private sector participation through tax benefits, grants, and subsidies for sustainable practices. International agreements, such as the Kunming-Montreal Global Biodiversity Framework, rely heavily on government action to meet global conservation targets.

Private Sector Involvement

The private sector has the financial capacity and innovative potential to drive impactful environmental initiatives. Businesses can invest in restoration projects through carbon offset programs, sustainable supply chains, and corporate social responsibility (CSR) initiatives. For example, companies in the agriculture and energy sectors can adopt nature-based solutions that align profitability with environmental goals. By integrating sustainability into their operations, private enterprises not only contribute to ecosystem health but also enhance their market reputation and resilience to environmental risks.

Community Engagement

Local communities are critical stakeholders in restoration projects, as they are often the most directly impacted by environmental changes. Community involvement ensures that initiatives are culturally relevant, socially equitable, and aligned with local needs. Indigenous and rural communities, in particular, possess valuable traditional knowledge and experience that can enhance conservation outcomes. Empowering these groups through capacity-building programs and benefit-sharing mechanisms fosters long-term stewardship and trust.

Collaborative Models in Action

Successful restoration efforts often arise from partnerships that integrate these stakeholders. Public-private partnerships (PPPs) can pool resources and share risks, enabling large-scale projects that neither sector could accomplish alone. For example, mangrove restoration projects often combine government funding, corporate investment, and community labor to rebuild coastal ecosystems. Similarly, co-management agreements, where communities and governments jointly manage protected areas, have proven effective in ensuring both ecological and social benefits.

The Path Forward

Collaborations between public, private, and community stakeholders are vital for achieving a NPE. By leveraging their combined strengths, these partnerships can address funding gaps, enhance project efficiency, and ensure inclusive participation. This collaborative approach fosters innovative, scalable solutions that balance economic growth with environmental restoration, creating sustainable outcomes for people and the planet.

A Vision for Large-Scale Restoration

Large-scale restoration envisions a future where degraded ecosystems are revitalized to support biodiversity, combat climate change, and sustain human wellbeing, creating a healthier and more resilient planet.

Future Goals and Ambitious Restoration Targets

The vision for large-scale restoration is centered around achieving ambitious global targets to reverse environmental degradation and restore ecosystems. These goals are vital for addressing biodiversity loss, mitigating climate change, and supporting sustainable development. One of the most prominent targets is the Kunming-Montreal Global Biodiversity Framework, which aims to protect and restore 30% of the planet's land and ocean areas by 2030. Known as the "30x30" target, this goal represents a global commitment to preserving critical ecosystems and enhancing their capacity to provide essential services.

Beyond protected areas, restoration initiatives are increasingly focused on specific ecosystems. For instance, global efforts to restore forests under the Bonn Challenge aim to bring 350 million hectares of deforested and degraded landscapes into restoration by 2030. This initiative not only enhances biodiversity but also contributes to carbon sequestration and soil fertility, benefiting both the environment and local communities.

Ambitious restoration targets also address aquatic ecosystems, such as wetlands, rivers, and coastal areas. Wetland restoration projects aim to recover vital habitats that regulate water cycles, support fisheries, and store carbon. Similarly, mangrove and coral reef restoration are key priorities for protecting coastal communities from storm surges and preserving marine biodiversity.

Achieving these restoration goals requires coordinated efforts across multiple stakeholders, including governments, businesses, and local communities. Investments in innovative technologies, such as drone-based tree planting and satellite monitoring, can accelerate restoration processes and ensure accountability. Additionally, financial mechanisms like carbon credits and public-private partnerships play a critical role in scaling up restoration efforts.

These ambitious targets represent a collective commitment to repairing the planet's natural systems. By pursuing these goals, we can create a future where restored ecosystems not only thrive but also contribute to global resilience, sustainable development, and the well-being of future generations.

Integrating Technology and Traditional Methods

Combining modern technology with traditional ecological knowledge offers powerful solutions for large-scale ecosystem restoration. This integration leverages the strengths of both approaches, ensuring efficient, scalable, and culturally appropriate restoration practices that address diverse environmental challenges.

Technological advancements have revolutionized restoration efforts by improving precision, monitoring, and efficiency. For instance, drones are increasingly used to map degraded areas, plant seeds, and monitor restoration progress in hard-to-reach regions. Remote sensing and satellite imagery provide real-time data on deforestation, soil health, and biodiversity, enabling stakeholders to track changes and adapt strategies. Artificial intelligence and machine learning further enhance these capabilities by analyzing large datasets to predict outcomes and optimize restoration plans.

Traditional ecological knowledge, held by indigenous and local communities, complements these technological tools by offering context-specific insights. This knowledge is rooted in generations of close observation and interaction with local ecosystems. For example, traditional methods of land management, such as controlled burns or agroforestry, are often more sustainable and effective than modern practices. These approaches not only conserve resources but also maintain cultural heritage and community engagement.

Integrating technology with traditional methods ensures that restoration efforts are both innovative and grounded in local realities. This synergy enhances the success of projects, creating resilient ecosystems that benefit both nature and the communities that depend on them.

Chapter 2: Halting and Reversing Biodiversity Loss

Biodiversity loss poses a critical threat to the health of ecosystems, the stability of economies, and the wellbeing of societies worldwide. As species and habitats continue to disappear at alarming rates, the need for transformative action becomes increasingly urgent. This chapter explores the causes and consequences of biodiversity decline, highlighting its far-reaching impacts on ecosystems and human life. It examines the frameworks, policies, and technological innovations that can halt and reverse this trend, emphasizing the importance of collaborative efforts among governments, businesses, and communities. By addressing biodiversity loss, we can build a more resilient, sustainable, and balanced future.

Understanding Biodiversity Loss

Understanding biodiversity loss is crucial for addressing its causes, mitigating its impacts, and developing effective strategies to protect the ecosystems that sustain life on Earth.

Causes: habitat loss, pollution, climate change, and invasive species

Biodiversity loss is driven by several interconnected factors, each contributing to the decline of ecosystems and species. Among these, habitat loss, pollution, climate change, and invasive species are the most significant and widespread causes.

Habitat Loss

Habitat loss is the leading driver of biodiversity decline. Activities such as deforestation, urban expansion, agricultural intensification, and mining result in the destruction and fragmentation of ecosystems. Forests, wetlands, and grasslands are particularly vulnerable, as they are often converted into farmland or urban developments. Fragmentation isolates species populations, reducing genetic diversity and making it harder for them to survive environmental changes. Without access to suitable habitats, many species face extinction.

Pollution

Pollution poses a significant threat to biodiversity, impacting ecosystems and species health. Industrial waste, agricultural runoff, plastic pollution, and chemical spills contaminate soil, water, and air. For instance, pesticides and fertilizers in waterways lead to algal blooms and oxygen depletion, causing the collapse of aquatic ecosystems. Plastic waste, ingested by marine animals, results in injury, starvation, and death. Persistent pollutants such as heavy metals and microplastics accumulate in food chains, threatening species at every trophic level.

Climate Change

Climate change exacerbates biodiversity loss by altering habitats and species' ability to adapt. Rising temperatures, shifting precipitation patterns, and more frequent extreme weather events disrupt ecosystems and force species to migrate, often with limited success. Coral reefs, for example, are highly sensitive to warming oceans, with widespread bleaching threatening marine biodiversity. Additionally, climate change accelerates habitat loss through desertification, melting ice caps, and rising sea levels, further endangering vulnerable species.

Invasive Species

The introduction of invasive species disrupts native ecosystems by outcompeting, preying on, or spreading diseases to native species. Human activities, such as global trade and travel, have accelerated the spread of non-native species. For example, the introduction of the Burmese python to the Florida Everglades has decimated populations of native mammals, disrupting the local food web. Invasive plants can outcompete native vegetation, reducing habitat quality and altering ecosystem functions.

Addressing these causes requires urgent, coordinated action. Protecting habitats, reducing pollution, mitigating climate change, and controlling invasive species are critical steps in halting and reversing biodiversity loss. By tackling these drivers, we can preserve the ecosystems and species that sustain life on Earth.

Consequences for ecosystems and economies

Biodiversity loss has profound consequences for ecosystems and economies, disrupting the balance of natural systems and undermining the foundations of human prosperity. As species disappear and ecosystems degrade, their ability to provide essential services diminishes, leading to far-reaching environmental, social, and economic impacts.

Impacts on Ecosystems

Ecosystems rely on biodiversity to maintain their structure, function, and resilience. The loss of key species can trigger cascading effects, destabilizing entire ecosystems. For example, the extinction of pollinators such as bees and butterflies threatens the reproduction of plants, including crops, resulting in reduced food availability. Similarly, the decline of predator populations can lead to overpopulation of prey species, disrupting food webs and altering habitat dynamics.

Degraded ecosystems are less capable of performing vital functions such as carbon storage, water filtration, and soil fertility maintenance. Wetlands, forests, and coral reefs that are diminished by biodiversity loss struggle to protect communities from floods, droughts, and coastal erosion, increasing vulnerability to natural disasters.

Economic Consequences

The economic costs of biodiversity loss are immense. Sectors such as agriculture, fisheries, and forestry, which depend on healthy ecosystems, face declining productivity and profitability as biodiversity declines. For instance, overfishing and the collapse of marine ecosystems result in lost livelihoods for millions dependent on fisheries. Similarly, soil degradation caused by biodiversity loss in agricultural systems reduces crop yields, leading to higher food prices and greater food insecurity.

Moreover, biodiversity loss undermines industries such as tourism and pharmaceuticals, which rely on intact ecosystems and access to biological resources. The cumulative economic losses from ecosystem degradation often outweigh the costs of investing in conservation and restoration.

The interconnectedness of ecosystems and economies highlights the urgent need to address biodiversity loss. Protecting biodiversity is not only an environmental imperative but also a cornerstone of economic stability and human wellbeing.

Current trends and global impact

Biodiversity is declining at an alarming rate, with scientists warning that we are amid the planet's sixth mass extinction. Current trends reveal that species are disappearing up to 1,000 times faster than natural extinction rates due to human activities. The 2019 Global Assessment Report on Biodiversity and Ecosystem Services estimated that nearly one million species are at risk of extinction within decades if immediate action is not taken. This trend reflects widespread habitat loss, overexploitation of resources, pollution, climate change, and the introduction of invasive species.

Terrestrial Biodiversity

Land-based ecosystems have suffered extensive degradation, with deforestation and agricultural expansion driving habitat loss. Forests, which house over 80% of terrestrial species, are being cleared at unsustainable rates, leading to the collapse of ecosystems and the disappearance of species reliant on forest habitats. Grasslands and wetlands have also experienced dramatic reductions, further impacting biodiversity and ecosystem functions.

Marine and Freshwater Biodiversity

Marine ecosystems are under significant pressure from overfishing, pollution, and climate change. Coral reefs, home to a quarter of marine life, are particularly vulnerable, with nearly half already degraded due to warming oceans and acidification. Freshwater species are declining faster than those in terrestrial or marine environments, largely due to damming, pollution, and water overextraction.

Global Impact

The loss of biodiversity has severe implications for ecosystem services that underpin human survival. Reduced crop diversity, declining fisheries, and compromised water quality affect food security and livelihoods, particularly in vulnerable communities. Economically, biodiversity loss threatens industries such as agriculture, fisheries, and ecotourism, leading to significant financial losses globally.

The current trends emphasize the need for urgent, coordinated efforts to halt biodiversity loss. Reversing these impacts is critical for safeguarding ecosystems, securing economic stability, and ensuring a sustainable future for all.

Frameworks and Policies

Frameworks and policies provide the foundational tools and strategies needed to address biodiversity loss, guiding global, national, and local efforts toward conservation and sustainable development.

Global agreements: Kunming-Montreal Agreement, SDGs

Global agreements are essential for uniting nations in the fight against biodiversity loss, establishing shared goals, and fostering collaborative action. Two key frameworks—the Kunming-Montreal Global Biodiversity Framework and the SDGs—are pivotal in addressing the interconnected challenges of biodiversity conservation and sustainable development.

Kunming-Montreal Global Biodiversity Framework

Adopted in 2022 during the COP15 conference under the CBD, the Kunming-Montreal Agreement sets ambitious targets to halt biodiversity loss and restore ecosystems by 2030. Its flagship target, commonly referred to as "30x30," aims to protect 30% of the world's land and oceans by 2030. This framework also prioritizes reducing the extinction risk for threatened species and integrating biodiversity values into economic decision-making.

The agreement emphasizes the importance of mobilizing financial resources to achieve its goals, with commitments to increase funding for biodiversity conservation, particularly in developing countries. Additionally, it advocates for fair and equitable sharing of benefits from genetic resources and calls for the inclusion of indigenous and local communities in conservation efforts. By promoting a holistic approach to biodiversity, the Kunming-Montreal Agreement lays the groundwork for a NPE that aligns environmental sustainability with human wellbeing.

SDGs

The SDGs, adopted by the United Nations in 2015, serve as a universal framework for addressing global challenges, including poverty, inequality, and environmental degradation. Several SDGs directly address biodiversity conservation, including:

- SDG 14 (Life Below Water): Focuses on the sustainable management of marine resources, protection of marine ecosystems, and reduction of ocean pollution.
- SDG 15 (Life on Land): Aims to combat desertification, restore degraded land, halt deforestation, and protect biodiversity in terrestrial ecosystems.

Beyond these specific goals, the SDGs emphasize the interconnectedness of biodiversity with other aspects of sustainable development, such as food security (SDG 2), clean water (SDG 6), and climate action (SDG 13). Biodiversity underpins these goals by providing essential ecosystem services, such as pollination, water purification, and carbon storage.

Synergies Between the Agreements

The Kunming-Montreal Agreement and the SDGs complement each other, offering a comprehensive roadmap for tackling biodiversity loss and its broader implications. While the Kunming-Montreal framework focuses specifically on biodiversity targets, the SDGs provide a broader context for integrating these efforts into global sustainable development agendas.

Global Commitments for Local Action

Both agreements highlight the importance of translating global commitments into actionable policies at national and local levels. By leveraging these frameworks, nations can align their efforts, share resources, and build partnerships to address biodiversity loss effectively. These agreements represent a collective commitment to preserving the planet's biodiversity, ensuring ecological resilience, and securing a sustainable future for all.

Local and regional biodiversity action plans

Local and regional biodiversity action plans (BAPs) are critical tools for addressing biodiversity loss at scales where tangible, targeted interventions can have the greatest impact. These plans translate global frameworks, such as the Kunming-Montreal Global Biodiversity Framework and the SDGs, into actionable strategies tailored to the unique ecological, social, and economic contexts of specific areas.

Purpose and Scope of Biodiversity Action Plans

BAPs aim to conserve and restore biodiversity by identifying key threats, setting measurable targets, and implementing strategies that prioritize the protection of local ecosystems and species. These plans often focus on preserving critical habitats, reducing pollution, combating invasive species, and promoting sustainable land-use practices. By aligning conservation goals with local priorities, BAPs enable communities and governments to address biodiversity challenges effectively while fostering sustainable development.

Developing Local and Regional Plans

Developing a BAP begins with a comprehensive assessment of local biodiversity, including the status of species, habitats, and ecosystem services. This baseline data informs the identification of conservation priorities and the design of interventions. Stakeholder engagement is a cornerstone of this process, ensuring that the voices of local communities, indigenous groups, businesses, and policymakers are considered. Collaborative decision-making helps balance ecological needs with social and economic interests.

BAPs also incorporate monitoring and evaluation frameworks to measure progress and adapt strategies as needed. Regular reporting and data collection ensure accountability and provide insights into the effectiveness of conservation efforts, enabling continuous improvement.

Examples of Successful BAPs

One successful example is the UK's Biodiversity Action Plan, which has been instrumental in protecting priority species and habitats across the country. By engaging local authorities, environmental organizations, and citizens, the plan has restored wetlands, increased pollinator populations, and preserved ancient woodlands. Similarly, regional initiatives in India focus on safeguarding biodiversity hotspots, such as the Western Ghats, by integrating traditional ecological knowledge with scientific approaches.

Benefits of Local and Regional Approaches

Local and regional BAPs provide the flexibility to address biodiversity challenges specific to a given area while contributing to broader conservation goals. These plans empower communities to take ownership of conservation efforts, fostering a sense of stewardship and ensuring that interventions are culturally and economically sustainable. Moreover, localized efforts can serve as models for broader replication, inspiring other regions to adopt similar strategies.

Role of NGOs and international organizations

Non-governmental organizations (NGOs) and international organizations play a pivotal role in addressing biodiversity loss, facilitating conservation efforts, and promoting sustainable development. These entities bridge the gap between global frameworks and local action, providing resources, expertise, and advocacy to ensure the protection and restoration of ecosystems worldwide.

Conservation Advocacy and Policy Influence

NGOs and international organizations are instrumental in shaping biodiversity policies and raising awareness about the importance of conservation. Through advocacy campaigns, they influence governments and industries to adopt sustainable practices and implement environmental protections. For example, organizations like the World Wildlife Fund (WWF) and Conservation International have been at the forefront of lobbying for ambitious global targets, such as the "30x30" goal under the Kunming-Montreal Global Biodiversity Framework.

These groups also play a critical role in holding governments and corporations accountable for their commitments to biodiversity and environmental sustainability. By monitoring progress, reporting violations, and proposing solutions, NGOs ensure that biodiversity goals remain a priority on the global agenda.

Capacity Building and Technical Support

NGOs and international organizations provide essential technical expertise and capacity-building programs to support local and regional conservation initiatives. They offer training, funding, and tools to governments, communities, and other stakeholders, enabling them to implement effective biodiversity action plans. For instance, organizations like BirdLife International and the International Union for Conservation of Nature (IUCN) provide data and research that guide the protection of critical habitats and endangered species.

Moreover, these organizations facilitate the transfer of knowledge and best practices across regions, fostering innovation and collaboration in biodiversity conservation. Their global networks enable the sharing of resources and expertise, ensuring that successful strategies are adapted and replicated in diverse contexts.

Direct Conservation Action

NGOs and international organizations are often involved in hands-on conservation work, from habitat restoration to species recovery programs. They lead efforts to reforest degraded landscapes, protect marine ecosystems, and combat wildlife trafficking. For example, the Nature Conservancy works globally to restore wetlands, coral reefs, and forests, while Wildlife Conservation Society (WCS) focuses on protecting wildlife populations and their habitats.

Community Engagement and Partnerships

A key strength of NGOs and international organizations lies in their ability to engage local communities and foster partnerships. By working closely with indigenous peoples and local stakeholders, they ensure that conservation efforts are inclusive and culturally appropriate. These collaborations not only enhance biodiversity outcomes but also improve social and economic resilience.

Global Coordination and Funding

International organizations like the United Nations Environment Programme (UNEP) and the Global Environment Facility (GEF) play a vital role in coordinating global efforts and mobilizing funding for biodiversity initiatives. Their programs connect governments, NGOs, and private sectors, driving large-scale conservation projects and addressing transboundary challenges.

Role of Technology

Technology plays a vital role in biodiversity conservation, offering innovative tools and solutions to monitor ecosystems, protect species, and support sustainable resource management.

AI and machine learning for tracking biodiversity.

Artificial intelligence (AI) and machine learning are transforming biodiversity conservation by providing powerful tools to monitor ecosystems, analyze data, and predict environmental changes. These technologies enable researchers and conservationists to gather and interpret vast amounts of information efficiently, leading to more effective and targeted conservation strategies.

Data Collection and Analysis

AI-powered tools are revolutionizing the way biodiversity data is collected and analyzed. For example, automated cameras and audio sensors equipped with AI can identify species based on images, sounds, or movements. These tools can process large datasets in real-time, detecting species that might otherwise be overlooked. For instance, AI algorithms have been used to identify bird calls in dense forests or monitor the movements of elusive mammals like tigers and leopards.

Machine learning models also help analyze satellite and drone imagery to map habitats, track deforestation, and monitor changes in ecosystems. These models can detect patterns and anomalies that indicate habitat degradation or species loss, providing critical insights to guide conservation efforts. By automating these processes, AI reduces the time and resources required for fieldwork while improving the accuracy and scope of monitoring.

Predictive Modeling

AI and machine learning are invaluable for predictive modeling, which assesses the future impacts of environmental changes on biodiversity. These models can simulate scenarios such as climate change, habitat loss, or the introduction of invasive species, allowing conservationists to develop proactive strategies. For instance, AI tools have been used to predict the spread of diseases among wildlife populations or forecast the impacts of rising temperatures on species distributions.

Community Science and Public Engagement

AI also facilitates community science initiatives by enabling citizen participation in biodiversity monitoring. Apps powered by AI, such as iNaturalist, allow users to upload photos of plants and animals, which are then identified and logged in biodiversity databases. This democratization of data collection expands the reach of conservation efforts and raises public awareness about the importance of protecting biodiversity.

Challenges and Opportunities

Despite its benefits, the use of AI in biodiversity tracking comes with challenges, including the need for reliable data inputs, computational resources, and ethical considerations related to privacy and data ownership. However, ongoing advancements in technology and collaborative efforts between governments, NGOs, and tech companies are addressing these challenges, unlocking new opportunities for AI-driven conservation.

AI and machine learning are powerful allies in the fight against biodiversity loss, enabling more efficient, accurate, and scalable monitoring of ecosystems. By harnessing these technologies, we can better understand and protect the natural world.

Drones and remote sensing for monitoring habitats

Drones and remote sensing technologies have become indispensable tools in monitoring habitats, providing high-resolution data and real-time insights into ecosystem health. These technologies offer cost-effective and efficient ways to assess large and inaccessible areas, revolutionizing the field of biodiversity conservation.

Drones for Habitat Monitoring

Drones, or unmanned aerial vehicles (UAVs), are increasingly used to survey habitats, monitor wildlife, and detect environmental changes. Equipped with cameras, thermal sensors, and LiDAR technology, drones can capture detailed images and data from diverse ecosystems, including forests, wetlands, and coastal areas. Unlike traditional ground-based methods, drones can quickly cover large areas, making them ideal for tracking changes in habitat conditions over time.

For instance, drones have been used to map deforestation, monitor coral reef health, and detect illegal logging and poaching activities. Thermal imaging sensors on drones can identify animal populations in dense forests or during nighttime surveys, aiding in species conservation efforts.

Remote Sensing for Ecosystem Analysis

Remote sensing technologies, such as satellite imagery and aerial photography, provide a broader perspective on habitat conditions and environmental changes. Satellites equipped with advanced sensors can detect changes in vegetation cover, water quality, and land use, offering valuable insights into ecosystem health. For example, remote sensing data is used to monitor desertification, map forest fires, and assess the impacts of climate change on habitats.

Benefits and Challenges

Both drones and remote sensing technologies enable conservationists to identify threats, prioritize restoration efforts, and track the effectiveness of interventions. However, challenges such as high initial costs, data interpretation requirements, and limited access to cutting-edge technology in some regions need to be addressed.

By combining drones and remote sensing, conservationists can monitor habitats more effectively, ensuring timely action to protect and restore ecosystems.

Citizen science and participatory technology

Citizen science and participatory technology empower individuals and communities to actively engage in biodiversity monitoring and conservation. These approaches leverage widespread access to technology, such as smartphones and apps, to collect valuable data, raise awareness, and foster a sense of stewardship for the environment.

Citizen Science Initiatives

Citizen science projects invite non-professionals to contribute to biodiversity research by observing and documenting species in their local environments. Platforms like iNaturalist, eBird, and PlantNet enable users to upload photographs, sounds, and other observations of wildlife, which are then identified and logged into global biodiversity databases. These initiatives provide researchers with large datasets that would otherwise be challenging and expensive to gather. For example, citizen-generated data has been instrumental in tracking migratory bird patterns, mapping invasive species, and monitoring seasonal changes in plant life.

Participatory Technology

Advances in participatory technology, such as AI-powered identification apps and GPS-enabled tools, enhance the effectiveness of citizen science. These technologies simplify the data collection process, allowing users to contribute without requiring extensive technical knowledge. For instance, smartphone apps can automatically identify species from photos, record geographic locations, and synchronize observations with centralized databases, ensuring accuracy and accessibility for researchers.

Community Engagement and Education

Citizen science fosters public engagement by connecting individuals to the natural world and increasing their understanding of biodiversity. Participatory technology bridges the gap between researchers and the public, creating opportunities for collaboration and shared responsibility in conservation efforts. This inclusivity helps build community support for environmental initiatives and strengthens local capacity to protect ecosystems.

By democratizing biodiversity monitoring, citizen science and participatory technology not only expand the reach of conservation efforts but also inspire broader societal commitment to preserving the planet's natural resources.

Engaging Stakeholders

Engaging stakeholders is essential for successful biodiversity conservation, as collaboration among governments, businesses, communities, and organizations ensures inclusive, effective, and sustainable outcomes.

Role of businesses in biodiversity conservation

Businesses play a critical role in biodiversity conservation by integrating sustainable practices into their operations and supply chains, reducing environmental impacts, and contributing to ecosystem restoration. As significant drivers of resource use and environmental change, businesses have both a responsibility and an opportunity to protect biodiversity while enhancing their long-term resilience and profitability.

One of the key ways businesses can support conservation is by adopting sustainable sourcing practices. For example, companies in agriculture, forestry, and fisheries can ensure their operations avoid deforestation, overfishing, or habitat destruction by using certified sustainable resources. Implementing circular economy models, which prioritize reducing waste and reusing materials, further minimizes harm to ecosystems.

Additionally, businesses can invest in biodiversity offsets and nature-based solutions to mitigate their environmental footprints. This includes funding reforestation projects, wetland restoration, or coral reef recovery to compensate for unavoidable impacts. By integrating biodiversity conservation into CSR programs, companies can demonstrate their commitment to environmental stewardship and build trust with stakeholders.

Partnerships with governments, NGOs, and communities allow businesses to contribute to large-scale conservation initiatives while benefiting from shared expertise and resources. Through innovation, funding, and responsible practices, businesses are essential collaborators in achieving global biodiversity goals.

Community engagement and education

Community engagement and education are vital components of successful biodiversity conservation, ensuring that local populations actively participate in protecting and restoring ecosystems. Communities often have the closest connection to natural environments, making their involvement essential for long-term conservation efforts.

Engaging communities begins with recognizing their knowledge, needs, and cultural values. Local and indigenous knowledge provides valuable insights into sustainable practices and the ecological dynamics of specific regions. Including communities in conservation planning and decision-making fosters a sense of ownership, ensuring that initiatives align with their priorities and gain lasting support. Participatory approaches, such as community-led monitoring and management programs, empower local populations to become stewards of biodiversity.

Education is another powerful tool for driving engagement. Raising awareness about the importance of biodiversity and the threats it faces encourages communities to adopt sustainable practices. Schools, workshops, and public campaigns can educate people about conservation methods, such as reducing waste, avoiding harmful pesticides, and protecting local habitats. Digital tools, like apps and social media, further amplify conservation messages and make them accessible to broader audiences.

By integrating community engagement and education into biodiversity initiatives, conservation efforts become more inclusive, sustainable, and effective. Empowered communities are better equipped to protect ecosystems, ensuring biodiversity thrives for generations to come.

Partnerships between governments and private entities

Partnerships between governments and private entities are essential for achieving large-scale biodiversity conservation. Governments provide regulatory frameworks, policies, and funding, while private entities contribute financial resources, innovation, and expertise. These collaborations enable impactful initiatives, such as reforestation projects, habitat restoration, and sustainable land management. For example, public-private partnerships (PPPs) can support carbon offset programs or fund biodiversity corridors, combining public oversight with private investment. By aligning conservation goals with economic incentives, these partnerships drive scalable, sustainable solutions. Such collaboration fosters shared responsibility, leveraging the strengths of both sectors to protect biodiversity and ensure long-term ecological and economic resilience.

Chapter 3: Creating Jobs in Nature Recovery

Nature recovery offers immense potential to create jobs while addressing critical environmental challenges. As ecosystems are restored and biodiversity is protected, opportunities emerge across sectors such as conservation, renewable energy, sustainable agriculture, and ecotourism. This chapter explores the economic benefits of investing in nature recovery, the industries driving green job creation, and the skills and training needed to build a nature-positive workforce. By linking environmental restoration with employment opportunities, nature recovery contributes to both ecological resilience and social equity, paving the way for a sustainable and inclusive economy.

Economic Opportunities in Nature Recovery

Nature recovery presents significant economic opportunities by creating green jobs, driving innovation, and supporting sustainable industries that align environmental restoration with long-term economic growth.

Overview of green jobs and their significance

Green jobs are a cornerstone of the transition to a sustainable economy, offering employment opportunities that support environmental restoration, biodiversity conservation, and climate resilience. These jobs span diverse sectors, including renewable energy, sustainable agriculture, conservation, and eco-friendly construction, and are integral to aligning economic growth with environmental stewardship.

What Are Green Jobs?

Green jobs are defined as roles that contribute to preserving or restoring the environment, whether through direct conservation activities or by reducing environmental impacts in other industries. Examples include reforestation workers, renewable energy technicians, biodiversity researchers, and sustainable urban planners. These jobs not only address critical environmental challenges but also create pathways for economic growth and stability.

Significance of Green Jobs

Green jobs play a vital role in fostering a NPE by creating a workforce dedicated to restoring ecosystems and building sustainable systems. They provide solutions to urgent global challenges, such as climate change and biodiversity loss, while supporting livelihoods and reducing economic inequality. In many cases, green jobs also serve as an entry point for developing countries to participate in global sustainability efforts, offering long-term economic benefits.

Moreover, green jobs have the potential to drive innovation and technological advancement. For instance, roles in renewable energy or sustainable farming often lead to the development of new methods and tools that improve efficiency and reduce environmental harm. As these industries expand, they contribute to job creation, economic diversification, and resilience.

Investing in green jobs is a win-win for the environment and the economy, fostering a future where human activities and natural systems coexist sustainably. By prioritizing these roles, we can accelerate the transition to a greener, more equitable world.

Economic benefits of investing in nature recovery

Investing in nature recovery yields significant economic benefits by creating jobs, stimulating local economies, and reducing long-term costs associated with environmental degradation. These investments not only contribute to biodiversity conservation and ecosystem restoration but also provide a foundation for sustainable economic growth and resilience.

Job Creation and Economic Growth

Nature recovery projects generate employment across multiple sectors, from reforestation and habitat restoration to sustainable agriculture and renewable energy. For instance, reforestation efforts require a diverse workforce, including tree planters, ecologists, and project managers. These jobs, often created in rural and underserved areas, provide stable livelihoods and reduce economic inequality. Furthermore, the development of industries such as ecotourism and sustainable fisheries boosts local economies by creating new revenue streams and supporting small businesses.

Cost Savings from Ecosystem Services

Healthy ecosystems provide critical services such as clean air, water filtration, and flood protection, which reduce the need for expensive infrastructure and disaster mitigation measures. For example, restoring wetlands can lower flood risks, saving millions in potential damages and reducing reliance on costly engineered solutions. Similarly, investing in coral reef restoration supports marine biodiversity and protects coastal communities from storm surges, avoiding significant economic losses.

Boosting Innovation and Economic Resilience

Nature recovery drives innovation in green technologies and sustainable practices. For example, advancements in renewable energy, water management, and sustainable farming methods emerge as industries adapt to support restoration goals. These innovations not only improve efficiency but also create new markets and opportunities for economic diversification. Additionally, nature-based solutions enhance resilience to climate change impacts, reducing economic vulnerabilities and fostering long-term stability.

Global Economic Impact

On a global scale, investing in nature recovery contributes to achieving international targets such as the SDGs and the Kunming-Montreal Global Biodiversity Framework. These efforts unlock funding opportunities, attract private sector investment, and strengthen international cooperation, further amplifying economic benefits.

In conclusion, investing in nature recovery is not only an environmental imperative but also an economic opportunity. By prioritizing ecosystem restoration, governments, businesses, and communities can secure sustainable growth, create jobs, and build resilience, ensuring a healthier and more prosperous future for all.

Key sectors driving nature-positive employment

Nature-positive employment spans diverse sectors that prioritize environmental restoration, biodiversity conservation, and sustainable practices. These sectors not only address pressing ecological challenges but also create stable and meaningful job opportunities, supporting the transition to a NPE.

Conservation and Restoration

The conservation sector employs professionals involved in protecting natural habitats, restoring ecosystems, and managing biodiversity. Roles include park rangers, ecologists, wildlife biologists, and reforestation workers. Large-scale restoration projects, such as wetland rehabilitation or mangrove reforestation, provide job opportunities for both skilled and unskilled workers, particularly in rural areas.

Renewable Energy

The renewable energy sector is a significant driver of green jobs, offering employment in wind, solar, hydropower, and geothermal energy projects. Transitioning to clean energy not only reduces greenhouse gas emissions but also creates a workforce dedicated to sustainable energy solutions. Jobs in this sector include engineers, technicians, and project managers, who play a crucial role in supporting global climate goals.

Sustainable Agriculture and Forestry

Agriculture and forestry sectors are key contributors to nature-positive employment through sustainable practices such as agroforestry, organic farming, and regenerative agriculture. These approaches improve soil health, enhance biodiversity, and reduce environmental impacts, creating jobs for farmers, agronomists, and forestry workers.

Ecotourism and Sustainable Tourism

Ecotourism offers a growing market for nature-positive employment, particularly in biodiversity-rich regions. Jobs in this sector include tour guides, hospitality staff, and conservation educators, all of whom support tourism that promotes environmental stewardship and cultural preservation.

Circular Economy

The circular economy drives employment by emphasizing waste reduction, recycling, and resource efficiency. Workers in this sector contribute to sustainable manufacturing, repair services, and material recovery, supporting the shift away from traditional linear production models.

By investing in these sectors, governments and businesses can drive economic growth while fostering environmental sustainability and resilience.

Key Industries for Employment Growth

Key industries driving employment growth in nature recovery include conservation, renewable energy, sustainable agriculture, ecotourism, and the circular economy, offering diverse opportunities to align economic development with environmental sustainability.

Conservation and land management

Conservation and land management are critical sectors driving employment growth in nature recovery, offering a range of opportunities to protect, restore, and sustainably manage natural ecosystems. These sectors play a central role in maintaining biodiversity, mitigating climate change, and ensuring the long-term health of landscapes, creating stable and meaningful jobs across diverse roles.

Protecting Natural Areas

Jobs in conservation focus on safeguarding ecosystems such as forests, wetlands, grasslands, and marine environments. Roles include park rangers, wildlife biologists, conservation officers, and habitat restoration specialists. These professionals work to preserve biodiversity by enforcing environmental regulations, monitoring wildlife populations, and managing protected areas. For instance, park rangers ensure the safety of national parks and nature reserves, protecting them from illegal activities like poaching and logging while educating visitors about the importance of conservation.

Restoration Projects

Land management plays a vital role in ecosystem restoration, creating employment opportunities in projects aimed at rehabilitating degraded landscapes. Workers are employed to plant trees, restore wetlands, and remove invasive species, while ecologists and project managers oversee planning and implementation. Large-scale restoration efforts, such as reforestation initiatives under the Bonn Challenge, provide both skilled and unskilled jobs, benefiting rural and underserved communities.

Sustainable Land Use Practices

Sustainable land management incorporates practices that balance ecological conservation with economic productivity. Jobs in this area focus on managing land for multiple uses, including agriculture, forestry, and recreation, while minimizing environmental impacts. Agroforestry workers, for example, integrate trees into farmland to enhance biodiversity, improve soil health, and increase yields. Similarly, sustainable forestry workers manage timber harvesting in ways that ensure forest regeneration and biodiversity preservation.

Innovative Technology in Land Management

Advancements in technology are creating new opportunities within the conservation and land management sectors. Geographic information systems (GIS) specialists and drone operators are increasingly employed to map landscapes, monitor environmental changes, and support restoration projects. These tools enable conservationists to collect data efficiently and make informed decisions about land management strategies.

Economic and Social Benefits

The conservation and land management sectors not only create jobs but also generate economic benefits by enhancing ecosystem services such as water filtration, flood protection, and carbon sequestration. Additionally, these jobs contribute to community development by providing training, income, and stability in regions that rely heavily on natural resources.

Ecotourism and sustainable travel

Ecotourism and sustainable travel are rapidly growing sectors that create jobs while promoting environmental conservation and cultural preservation. These industries align economic development with nature recovery, offering meaningful employment opportunities while fostering global awareness of biodiversity and sustainability.

What is Ecotourism?

Ecotourism is a form of responsible travel that focuses on visiting natural areas while conserving the environment and benefiting local communities. Unlike conventional tourism, ecotourism emphasizes low-impact activities, such as wildlife observation, hiking, and cultural experiences, that support conservation efforts. Sustainable travel, a broader concept, includes minimizing carbon footprints, supporting eco-friendly accommodations, and encouraging ethical travel practices.

Jobs in Ecotourism

Ecotourism generates employment across a wide range of roles, particularly in biodiversity-rich regions. Tour guides and naturalists are critical for leading eco-friendly excursions and educating visitors about local ecosystems and conservation efforts. Hospitality staff at eco-lodges and sustainable resorts contribute to the industry by providing accommodations that prioritize energy efficiency and waste reduction. Conservation educators and interpreters work with visitors to raise awareness about environmental issues and promote sustainable practices. Additionally, local artisans and food producers benefit from ecotourism by supplying culturally significant goods and services to travelers.

Benefits to Conservation and Communities

Ecotourism directly supports conservation initiatives by generating revenue that funds the protection and restoration of natural areas. Entrance fees, donations, and a percentage of tourism profits often go toward maintaining national parks, wildlife reserves, and marine sanctuaries. For example, gorilla trekking tours in Rwanda and Uganda fund habitat preservation and anti-poaching efforts.

Local communities also benefit from ecotourism through job creation and income generation. By prioritizing community involvement, ecotourism empowers indigenous and rural populations to take ownership of conservation projects. Programs that train local guides and support community-run eco-lodges ensure that tourism revenue stays within the region, fostering economic stability and social equity.

Sustainable Travel Practices

The sustainable travel sector encourages businesses and travelers to adopt eco-friendly practices. This includes using renewable energy, minimizing single-use plastics, and promoting carbon-offset programs. For example, airlines and travel companies are increasingly offering carbon-neutral options, and eco-certifications help travelers identify accommodations that meet sustainability standards.

Challenges and Opportunities

Despite its benefits, ecotourism faces challenges such as overcrowding, habitat disturbance, and the risk of "greenwashing" by businesses falsely marketing themselves as sustainable. To address these issues, stricter regulations, transparent certifications, and visitor education are essential.

Renewable energy and nature-based solutions

The renewable energy sector and nature-based solutions (NbS) are pivotal in creating jobs and addressing climate and biodiversity challenges. These industries offer sustainable alternatives to fossil fuels while restoring ecosystems and supporting local communities, making them essential components of a NPE.

Renewable Energy: Driving Green Employment

The renewable energy sector, encompassing solar, wind, hydropower, and geothermal energy, is a major driver of green jobs. As countries transition to clean energy systems, opportunities for employment span installation, maintenance, research, and development. Solar panel technicians, wind turbine engineers, and project managers are among the many roles that contribute to the rapid growth of this sector. For instance, the International Renewable Energy Agency (IRENA) estimates that the renewable energy industry could employ over 38 million people globally by 2030.

Renewable energy projects also support biodiversity by reducing the environmental impacts of traditional energy systems. For example, offshore wind farms can create artificial reefs that enhance marine biodiversity. Additionally, integrating renewable energy systems with sustainable land management practices can help restore degraded areas while generating clean power.

Nature-Based Solutions: Restoring Ecosystems

Nature-based solutions involve using natural processes to address environmental challenges, such as climate change, water security, and biodiversity loss. Examples include reforestation, wetland restoration, and mangrove planting, all of which create jobs while delivering environmental benefits. Workers in NbS projects are employed in activities such as tree planting, habitat restoration, and community engagement.

Reforestation projects not only absorb carbon dioxide but also provide critical habitats for wildlife and support sustainable livelihoods for local communities. Mangrove restoration, a key NbS initiative, protects coastal areas from storm surges, reduces erosion, and enhances fishery resources, creating jobs in both conservation and sustainable aquaculture.

Economic and Environmental Benefits

Investing in renewable energy and NbS generates long-term economic benefits by creating stable, high-quality jobs and reducing costs associated with environmental degradation. For example, reforestation reduces flood risks and improves water quality, lowering infrastructure and healthcare costs. Similarly, renewable energy reduces reliance on fossil fuels, mitigating climate impacts and enhancing energy security.

Challenges and Collaboration

Scaling up renewable energy and NbS requires overcoming challenges such as high upfront costs, regulatory barriers, and the need for skilled labor. Collaboration among governments, businesses, and communities is essential to address these issues. Public-private partnerships and international funding mechanisms can help mobilize resources and expertise, ensuring that these industries reach their full potential.

Building a Nature-Positive Workforce

Building a nature-positive workforce requires equipping individuals with the skills, knowledge, and opportunities needed to drive sustainable practices and restore ecosystems across various industries.

Education and training programs for green jobs

Education and training programs are essential for developing the workforce needed to support the transition to a NPE. These programs equip individuals with the skills and knowledge required to fill roles in conservation, renewable energy, sustainable agriculture, and other green industries, ensuring that job creation aligns with environmental and economic goals.

Specialized Education for Green Careers

Formal education plays a key role in preparing individuals for green jobs. Universities and technical institutions are increasingly offering programs focused on environmental science, renewable energy technologies, and sustainable resource management. Courses in areas such as conservation biology, climate change mitigation, and circular economy principles provide foundational knowledge for those entering nature-positive careers. For example, degrees in renewable energy engineering or sustainable agriculture equip graduates to design and implement solutions that address biodiversity loss and climate change.

Vocational Training and Certification

Vocational training programs and certifications are critical for providing hands-on, practical skills for green jobs. These programs are especially valuable for workers transitioning from traditional industries to emerging green sectors. For instance, certifications in solar panel installation, wildlife management, or organic farming prepare individuals for specialized roles, ensuring they meet industry standards. Short-term training programs also allow workers to quickly upskill or reskill, making green jobs more accessible.

Community-Based Training Initiatives

In rural and underserved areas, community-based training programs play a vital role in building local capacity for nature recovery. These initiatives often focus on practical skills like reforestation techniques, water management, or eco-tourism operations. By involving local populations, these programs foster community ownership of conservation efforts while creating employment opportunities.

Reskilling workers from traditional industries

Reskilling workers from traditional industries is essential to ensure a just transition toward a NPE. Many workers in sectors such as fossil fuels, manufacturing, and intensive agriculture face job displacement due to the global shift toward sustainability. Reskilling programs provide these workers with the tools and knowledge needed to transition into green jobs, supporting both their livelihoods and the broader goal of environmental restoration.

Identifying Transferable Skills

Workers in traditional industries often possess skills that can be adapted to nature-positive sectors. For example, mechanics and engineers in the oil and gas industry can transition into renewable energy roles, such as wind turbine maintenance or solar panel installation. Similarly, farmers accustomed to conventional practices can be trained in sustainable agriculture methods, such as regenerative farming or agroforestry, which prioritize soil health and biodiversity.

Customized Training Programs

Tailored reskilling programs are critical to helping workers make the transition. These programs focus on bridging the gap between existing expertise and the requirements of green jobs. For instance, courses in energy efficiency retrofitting enable construction workers to contribute to sustainable building projects, while workshops on habitat restoration teach skills like tree planting and invasive species management.

Supportive Policies and Collaboration

Government and private sector collaboration is key to scaling reskilling efforts. Public funding, incentives, and partnerships with educational institutions and businesses can create accessible training opportunities. For example, apprenticeship programs that combine classroom instruction with hands-on experience help workers build confidence and competence in new roles.

Leveraging partnerships with academic institutions

Partnerships with academic institutions play a vital role in building a skilled workforce for the NPE. Universities, colleges, and research centers provide the expertise, resources, and infrastructure needed to develop education and training programs tailored to emerging green industries. By collaborating with these institutions, governments, businesses, and organizations can create pathways for individuals to gain the knowledge and skills required for nature-positive careers.

Academic partnerships enable the development of specialized curricula in areas such as renewable energy, conservation biology, and sustainable agriculture. These collaborations also support research initiatives that advance innovative solutions for biodiversity conservation and ecosystem restoration. Internships, apprenticeships, and joint training programs connect students with real-world experience, bridging the gap between academia and industry.

Through these partnerships, academic institutions help foster a workforce equipped to address environmental challenges, ensuring that education and industry work together to achieve a sustainable and resilient future.

Opportunities in Developing Economies

Developing economies have significant opportunities to align nature recovery with economic growth, creating jobs and fostering sustainable development while addressing environmental challenges.

Integrating nature recovery with economic growth

Integrating nature recovery with economic growth provides developing economies with an opportunity to address environmental challenges while fostering sustainable development. Nature recovery projects, such as reforestation, wetland restoration, and sustainable agriculture, generate jobs and stimulate local economies. These initiatives not only restore ecosystems but also create long-term economic benefits by improving resource availability and resilience.

Sustainable land-use practices, such as agroforestry and regenerative agriculture, enhance soil fertility and water retention, leading to increased agricultural productivity and food security. Similarly, investments in ecotourism and renewable energy projects provide revenue streams that support both economic growth and conservation efforts.

By aligning restoration goals with development priorities, governments and businesses in developing economies can ensure that economic activities contribute to environmental health. This integrated approach attracts international funding and partnerships, further boosting economic opportunities while addressing global biodiversity and climate goals.

Supporting local and indigenous communities

Supporting local and indigenous communities is critical for the success of nature recovery initiatives, as these groups are often the most directly connected to and reliant on natural ecosystems. Empowering communities through training, resources, and equitable benefit-sharing ensures that conservation efforts align with their needs and knowledge. Indigenous practices, rooted in traditional ecological understanding, often provide sustainable solutions for managing ecosystems. By involving local populations in decision-making and offering opportunities in green jobs such as reforestation, eco-tourism, and sustainable agriculture, governments and organizations can foster stewardship, improve livelihoods, and ensure the long-term success of restoration projects.

Chapter 4: Helping Industries Adopt Sustainable Practices

Industries play a critical role in shaping environmental outcomes, making their transition to sustainable practices essential for achieving a NPE. This chapter explores the drivers and benefits of adopting sustainable models, the tools and frameworks industries can use, and the incentives and regulations that encourage change. By aligning business operations with environmental goals, industries can reduce their ecological footprint, enhance resilience, and contribute to biodiversity conservation and ecosystem restoration.

Why Industries Must Transition

Industries must transition to sustainable practices to mitigate environmental impacts, address growing regulatory and consumer pressures, and ensure long-term economic and ecological resilience.

Risks of unsustainable practices

Unsustainable industrial practices pose significant risks to the environment, economies, and societies, leading to long-term consequences that jeopardize both business viability and global ecological health.

Environmental Degradation

Industries that rely on unsustainable practices contribute heavily to environmental degradation. Overexploitation of natural resources, pollution, deforestation, and habitat destruction disrupt ecosystems, resulting in biodiversity loss and reduced ecosystem services such as clean water, carbon storage, and soil fertility. For instance, industrial emissions and improper waste disposal contribute to air and water pollution, harming wildlife and human health.

Economic Instability

Unsustainable practices expose industries to economic risks, including resource scarcity and rising operational costs. Overharvesting natural resources, such as fish stocks or timber, leads to supply chain disruptions and reduced productivity over time. Additionally, reliance on finite resources, like fossil fuels, increases vulnerability to market volatility and price spikes, undermining business stability.

Reputational Damage

As consumers, investors, and governments demand greater accountability, industries that fail to adopt sustainable practices face reputational risks. Public awareness of environmental issues has led to increased scrutiny of corporate activities, with businesses perceived as environmentally irresponsible often losing customer loyalty and market share. Negative publicity can also deter investors, impacting access to capital.

Regulatory and Legal Risks

Governments worldwide are introducing stricter environmental regulations and penalties for non-compliance. Industries that persist with unsustainable practices risk legal action, fines, and operational restrictions. For example, regulations on carbon emissions and waste management are becoming increasingly stringent, compelling businesses to adapt or face financial penalties.

Climate-Related Risks

Industries that contribute to climate change through greenhouse gas emissions or deforestation are increasingly vulnerable to its impacts. Extreme weather events, rising temperatures, and sea-level rise disrupt operations, damage infrastructure, and increase insurance costs. Businesses that fail to mitigate these risks may face significant financial losses and operational challenges.

Economic and environmental benefits of adopting NPE principles

Adopting NPE principles offers industries substantial economic and environmental benefits, enabling businesses to achieve sustainable growth while contributing to biodiversity conservation and ecosystem restoration.

Economic Benefits

1. Cost Savings: Sustainable practices reduce operational costs by improving resource efficiency and minimizing waste. For example, adopting circular economy models—such as recycling materials or using renewable energy—lowers expenses and enhances profitability.
2. Market Opportunities: NPE principles open new revenue streams by creating demand for eco-friendly products and services. Businesses that prioritize sustainability gain access to green markets and consumer segments that value environmentally responsible practices.
3. Resilience to Resource Scarcity: By adopting sustainable resource management strategies, industries reduce dependence on finite resources, ensuring long-term stability and mitigating risks associated with resource depletion.
4. Investor Confidence: Increasingly, investors favor companies that demonstrate commitment to environmental, social, and governance (ESG) criteria. Adopting NPE principles attracts sustainable financing and improves access to capital.
5. Job Creation: Transitioning to NPE-aligned practices fosters job creation in areas such as renewable energy, sustainable agriculture, and conservation, stimulating local economies and enhancing community wellbeing.

Environmental Benefits

- Biodiversity Conservation: NPE principles prioritize protecting and restoring ecosystems, helping industries minimize their ecological footprint. Sustainable supply chain practices, for instance, reduce habitat destruction and promote biodiversity.
- Climate Mitigation: Industries adopting renewable energy and low-carbon technologies significantly reduce greenhouse gas emissions, contributing to global climate goals and enhancing their resilience to climate-related disruptions.
- Pollution Reduction: Sustainable waste management practices, such as recycling and responsible disposal, reduce environmental pollution, protecting air, water, and soil quality.
- Enhanced Ecosystem Services: By restoring degraded habitats, industries ensure the continued provision of vital ecosystem services, including water purification, pollination, and flood control, which benefit both businesses and communities.

Public expectations and pressures for sustainability

Public expectations and pressures for sustainability are driving industries to adopt more environmentally responsible practices. Consumers, investors, and governments increasingly demand that businesses align their operations with sustainable principles, reflecting a broader societal shift toward environmental consciousness.

Consumer Demand

Today's consumers prioritize companies that demonstrate a commitment to sustainability. They actively seek eco-friendly products and services, often willing to pay a premium for goods that reduce environmental harm. Brands perceived as environmentally irresponsible face reputational risks, including loss of customer loyalty and market share. Public campaigns and boycotts against unsustainable practices further amplify this pressure.

Investor Focus

Investors are increasingly integrating ESG criteria into their decision-making processes. Companies that fail to meet sustainability standards risk losing access to capital and attracting negative attention from stakeholders. Sustainability-focused investments have grown substantially, reflecting investor preference for businesses that contribute to a NPE.

Regulatory Momentum

Governments worldwide are implementing stricter environmental regulations in response to public concerns about climate change and biodiversity loss. Businesses face mounting pressure to comply with these policies, which include emissions reduction targets, waste management requirements, and incentives for sustainable innovation.

Public expectations for sustainability are reshaping the business landscape, compelling industries to adopt practices that protect the environment while maintaining competitiveness.

Tools for Transformation

Tools for transformation provide industries with practical frameworks, technologies, and strategies to integrate sustainable practices, reduce their environmental footprint, and contribute to a NPE.

Life cycle assessments for sustainable production

Life Cycle Assessment (LCA) is a powerful tool that helps industries evaluate the environmental impacts of their products and processes from inception to disposal. By examining every stage of a product's life cycle—raw material extraction, manufacturing, distribution, use, and end-of-life management—LCA provides a comprehensive understanding of the ecological footprint associated with production.

This approach enables businesses to identify opportunities for improvement, reduce resource consumption, and adopt more sustainable practices.

Key Components of LCA

LCA involves four main steps:

1. Goal and Scope Definition: This phase defines the purpose of the assessment, the system boundaries, and the specific aspects of the product or process to be analyzed.
2. Inventory Analysis: Data is collected on inputs (e.g., raw materials, energy) and outputs (e.g., emissions, waste) across all life cycle stages.
3. Impact Assessment: The collected data is analyzed to evaluate environmental impacts, such as greenhouse gas emissions, water usage, and pollution levels.
4. Interpretation: The findings are reviewed to identify areas for improvement and guide decision-making toward sustainability goals.

Applications of LCA

LCA is widely used to enhance sustainability in industries such as manufacturing, construction, and agriculture. For example, in the packaging industry, LCA can compare the environmental impacts of plastic, glass, and biodegradable materials, guiding companies toward eco-friendly choices. In construction, LCAs help assess the carbon footprint of building materials, promoting the use of low-impact alternatives like recycled steel or sustainably sourced wood.

Benefits of LCA

- Improved Resource Efficiency: By identifying stages of high resource consumption or waste generation, LCA enables companies to optimize processes and reduce costs.

- Reduced Environmental Impact: LCA highlights areas where changes can significantly lower emissions, energy use, or pollution.
- Enhanced Product Design: Insights from LCA guide the development of sustainable products, such as energy-efficient appliances or recyclable packaging.
- Regulatory Compliance and Market Advantage: Conducting LCAs helps businesses meet environmental regulations and appeal to eco-conscious consumers, enhancing competitiveness.

Challenges and Opportunities

Despite its benefits, LCA can be resource-intensive, requiring detailed data collection and analysis. However, advancements in software tools and databases are making LCA more accessible and efficient for businesses of all sizes. Collaboration with external experts and stakeholders can further streamline the process.

Conclusion

Life Cycle Assessment is an invaluable tool for promoting sustainable production. By providing a detailed understanding of environmental impacts, LCA empowers businesses to make informed decisions, reduce their ecological footprint, and align with the principles of a NPE.

Certifications and eco-labeling

Certifications and eco-labeling are essential tools for industries transitioning to sustainable practices. These initiatives provide transparency, accountability, and consumer confidence by identifying products and services that meet specific environmental and social standards. By adopting certifications and eco-labels, businesses demonstrate their commitment to sustainability, gain a competitive edge, and contribute to the goals of a NPE.

What Are Certifications and Eco-Labels?

Certifications are third-party validations that confirm a product, process, or organization adheres to established environmental or social criteria. Eco-labels are visual symbols or markings that communicate this compliance to consumers. Examples include certifications like Fair Trade, Forest Stewardship Council (FSC), and LEED for green building, as well as eco-labels such as the Energy Star logo or the EU Ecolabel.

Benefits for Businesses and Consumers

- Market Differentiation: Certifications and eco-labels help businesses stand out in competitive markets by appealing to environmentally and socially conscious consumers.
- Consumer Trust: These labels provide assurance that a product or service meets high sustainability standards, enhancing brand credibility.
- Regulatory Compliance: Certifications often align with government regulations, helping businesses avoid legal risks and access international markets.
- Operational Efficiency: Achieving certification can uncover inefficiencies, prompting companies to optimize processes and reduce waste.

Examples of Leading Certifications

- Fair Trade Certification: Ensures that producers receive fair wages and work in safe conditions while promoting sustainable farming practices.
- FSC Certification: Guarantees that timber and paper products come from responsibly managed forests, protecting biodiversity and reducing deforestation.
- LEED Certification: Recognizes buildings that meet stringent energy efficiency and sustainability criteria, supporting the construction of eco-friendly infrastructure.

- ISO 14001: An international standard for environmental management systems, helping organizations minimize their environmental footprint.

Challenges and Criticism

Despite their benefits, certifications and eco-labels face challenges, including the risk of "greenwashing," where labels are misleading or lack rigorous enforcement. Additionally, the costs associated with certification processes can be prohibitive for small businesses. To address these issues, it is critical to ensure transparency, robust criteria, and accessible pathways for certification.

Future Opportunities

As consumer demand for sustainable products grows, certifications and eco-labeling are becoming increasingly influential. Governments and industry bodies can enhance their impact by supporting awareness campaigns, subsidizing certification costs for small businesses, and integrating these systems into regulatory frameworks.

Nature-based solutions for industry practices

NbS offer a transformative approach for industries to align their operations with environmental sustainability while addressing critical challenges like climate change, biodiversity loss, and resource depletion. By leveraging natural processes, industries can integrate NbS into their practices to restore ecosystems, enhance resilience, and reduce their ecological footprint.

What Are Nature-Based Solutions?

NbS are actions that work with nature to deliver environmental, social, and economic benefits. They involve protecting, restoring, or sustainably managing ecosystems to address specific challenges, such as carbon sequestration, water purification, or flood mitigation. Examples include reforestation, wetland restoration, green infrastructure, and agroforestry.

Applications in Industry

- Carbon Sequestration: Industries in the energy and manufacturing sectors can invest in reforestation and afforestation projects to offset their carbon emissions. Forest restoration absorbs atmospheric carbon dioxide while improving biodiversity and soil health.
- Water Management: NbS like wetland restoration and riparian buffer zones help industries manage water resources sustainably. For example, breweries and agricultural businesses can use constructed wetlands to filter wastewater, reducing pollution and protecting downstream ecosystems.
- Agriculture: Agroforestry practices integrate trees into farmland, enhancing soil fertility, water retention, and biodiversity. This approach benefits industries reliant on sustainable agricultural supply chains while improving resilience to climate impacts.
- Urban Development: Green infrastructure, such as green roofs, urban forests, and permeable pavements, helps construction and real estate sectors mitigate urban heat, manage stormwater, and enhance urban biodiversity.

Benefits of NbS for Industries

- Environmental Impact Reduction: NbS allow industries to address key environmental challenges, such as reducing emissions, improving water quality, and preventing soil erosion.
- Cost-Effectiveness: NbS often provide cost-effective alternatives to engineered solutions. For instance, restoring wetlands can be more affordable than building water treatment plants.

- Regulatory Compliance: As governments introduce stricter environmental regulations, NbS help industries meet sustainability targets and avoid penalties.
- Reputation and Market Advantage: Implementing NbS demonstrates corporate social responsibility, attracting environmentally conscious consumers and investors.

Challenges in Implementation

Despite their advantages, implementing NbS requires overcoming challenges such as initial investment costs, land-use conflicts, and the need for interdisciplinary expertise. Collaborative efforts between governments, businesses, and communities are essential to address these barriers and scale up NbS adoption.

Future Opportunities

The growing recognition of NbS in global frameworks, such as the Kunming-Montreal Global Biodiversity Framework and the Paris Agreement, underscores their potential for industries. Investments in NbS not only contribute to achieving sustainability goals but also create new markets for green jobs and technologies.

Examples of Industry Adoption

Examples of industry adoption highlight how businesses across various sectors are successfully integrating sustainable practices to align with NPE principles.

Sustainable agriculture

Sustainable agriculture is a cornerstone of the NPE, offering practices that balance food production with environmental preservation. By integrating techniques that prioritize ecosystem health, resource efficiency, and biodiversity conservation, sustainable agriculture addresses the environmental challenges posed by traditional farming while ensuring long-term productivity and food security.

Principles of Sustainable Agriculture

- Soil Health: Practices such as crop rotation, cover cropping, and reduced tillage maintain soil fertility, structure, and microbial activity, minimizing erosion and degradation. Healthy soils also enhance water retention and carbon storage, contributing to climate resilience.
- Efficient Resource Use: Sustainable agriculture emphasizes water conservation through techniques like drip irrigation and rainwater harvesting. It also promotes the efficient use of fertilizers and pesticides to reduce runoff and pollution.
- Biodiversity Conservation: Integrating biodiversity into farming systems, such as through agroforestry or buffer zones, supports pollinators, natural pest control, and resilient ecosystems.

Techniques and Innovations

- Agroforestry: By combining crops with trees, agroforestry systems enhance soil fertility, provide habitat for wildlife, and reduce greenhouse gas emissions.
- Organic Farming: Eliminating synthetic inputs, organic farming relies on natural fertilizers and pest control, reducing environmental impacts and promoting healthier ecosystems.
- Precision Agriculture: Leveraging technology like drones and sensors, precision agriculture optimizes resource use, monitors crop health, and minimizes waste, making farming more sustainable.

Economic and Environmental Benefits

Sustainable agriculture delivers numerous economic benefits, including reduced input costs, improved yields, and market opportunities for eco-certified products. Environmentally, it restores soil health, reduces greenhouse gas emissions, and safeguards water quality. For example, regenerative farming practices can sequester significant amounts of carbon in the soil, mitigating climate change while improving crop productivity.

Challenges and Solutions

Adopting sustainable practices requires overcoming challenges such as high initial costs, access to technology, and resistance to change. Governments and organizations can support this transition through subsidies, training programs, and market incentives for sustainable products.

Renewable energy and green technology

Renewable energy and green technology are at the forefront of sustainable industrial transformation, providing clean, efficient, and environmentally friendly alternatives to traditional energy systems and technologies. These innovations play a critical role in reducing greenhouse gas emissions, conserving resources, and driving economic growth within a NPE.

Renewable Energy Solutions

The shift from fossil fuels to renewable energy sources such as solar, wind, hydropower, and geothermal is essential for mitigating climate change and protecting biodiversity. Solar and wind energy, in particular, have seen rapid adoption due to falling costs and technological advancements. For example, solar panels can be integrated into rooftops and infrastructure, while offshore wind farms harness consistent wind patterns to generate clean electricity.

Bioenergy, derived from organic materials such as agricultural waste and algae, offers another sustainable solution. When combined with carbon capture and storage technologies, bioenergy can even achieve net-negative emissions, contributing to climate mitigation goals.

Green Technology Innovations

Green technologies enhance energy efficiency and resource management across industries. Examples include smart grids that optimize energy distribution, energy-efficient appliances, and sustainable construction materials. Advanced batteries and storage systems enable better integration of renewable energy into the grid, ensuring reliable supply.

Economic and Environmental Benefits

Renewable energy and green technology reduce dependence on finite resources, lower energy costs, and create millions of green jobs globally. Additionally, these solutions minimize air and water pollution, protect ecosystems from the impacts of resource extraction, and contribute to global climate goals.

Circular economy approaches in manufacturing

The circular economy transforms traditional manufacturing by focusing on reducing waste, maximizing resource efficiency, and designing products for durability, reuse, and recycling. Unlike the linear "take-make-dispose" model, the circular economy emphasizes closed-loop systems that extend the lifecycle of materials, reduce environmental impacts, and contribute to a NPE.

Key Principles of Circular Manufacturing

- Design for Durability and Reuse: Products are designed to last longer and be easily repaired, reused, or upgraded, minimizing the need for new materials.
- Resource Efficiency: Manufacturing processes prioritize reducing material inputs, energy consumption, and waste generation.

- Recycling and Upcycling: Materials from end-of-life products are recovered and reprocessed into new products, reducing reliance on virgin resources.
- Industrial Symbiosis: Waste from one manufacturing process becomes a resource for another, creating a network of sustainable production.

Applications in Manufacturing

Circular approaches are widely adopted in industries such as electronics, automotive, and textiles. For example, remanufacturing of electronic components reduces e-waste while conserving rare materials like cobalt and lithium. In the automotive industry, manufacturers recover and recycle metals and plastics from end-of-life vehicles to produce new parts. Similarly, textile companies use recycled fibers to create sustainable clothing lines.

Economic and Environmental Benefits

Circular manufacturing reduces production costs by reusing materials, lowers waste management expenses, and opens new market opportunities for sustainable products. Environmentally, it minimizes resource extraction, decreases landfill waste, and reduces greenhouse gas emissions, making manufacturing more sustainable.

Incentives and Regulations

Incentives and regulations are essential tools for driving industrial adoption of sustainable practices, ensuring compliance while encouraging innovation and investment in a NPE.

Tax benefits and subsidies for sustainable businesses

Tax benefits and subsidies are powerful incentives that encourage businesses to adopt sustainable practices, invest in green technologies, and transition toward a NPE. These financial mechanisms reduce the cost burden of implementing environmentally responsible strategies, fostering innovation and accelerating the shift to sustainability.

Tax Benefits

Governments offer tax incentives to reward businesses for their commitment to sustainability. Examples include tax credits for renewable energy installations, such as solar panels or wind turbines, and deductions for energy efficiency upgrades in buildings or manufacturing processes. Companies that engage in research and development (R&D) of green technologies may also qualify for tax breaks. For instance, businesses developing energy-efficient appliances or eco-friendly packaging often receive incentives to offset the costs of innovation.

Carbon tax exemptions or reductions further incentivize companies to reduce greenhouse gas emissions by transitioning to cleaner energy sources or adopting carbon capture technologies. These measures not only lower operational costs but also position businesses as leaders in environmental responsibility.

Subsidies

Subsidies directly support sustainable businesses by reducing the financial barriers to adopting green practices. For example, subsidies for renewable energy projects lower upfront installation costs, making technologies like solar and wind power more accessible to industries and small businesses. Similarly, grants for sustainable agriculture help farmers transition to regenerative practices that enhance biodiversity and soil health.

Governments also provide subsidies for circular economy initiatives, such as recycling infrastructure and waste-to-energy projects. These funds enable businesses to adopt resource-efficient models that align with global sustainability goals.

Regulatory frameworks encouraging sustainability

Regulatory frameworks play a vital role in promoting sustainability by setting clear standards and requirements for businesses to reduce their environmental impacts. These regulations create accountability, drive innovation, and ensure alignment with global environmental goals.

Emissions and Pollution Controls

Governments worldwide implement regulations to limit greenhouse gas emissions and control pollution. For instance, carbon pricing mechanisms, such as carbon taxes and cap-and-trade systems, incentivize industries to adopt cleaner energy sources and reduce emissions. Pollution control standards, such as those regulating wastewater discharge or air quality, ensure that industrial processes minimize harm to ecosystems and human health.

Sustainable Resource Management

Regulations also mandate sustainable use of natural resources. For example, laws governing deforestation and fisheries promote responsible sourcing and prevent overexploitation. Similarly, extended producer responsibility (EPR) policies require manufacturers to manage the lifecycle of their products, encouraging recycling and waste reduction.

Incentives for Compliance

Regulatory frameworks often include incentives, such as fast-track permits or tax benefits, for businesses that exceed compliance standards. These measures reward proactive efforts to innovate and adopt best practices.

Chapter 5: Conserving and Restoring Ecosystem Benefits

Conserving and restoring ecosystems is essential for maintaining the benefits they provide to humanity and the planet. From clean water and fertile soil to climate regulation and biodiversity, ecosystems underpin our wellbeing and economic stability. This chapter explores the critical services ecosystems deliver, the threats they face, and the strategies needed to conserve and restore their health, ensuring a sustainable future for all.

The Value of Ecosystem Services

Ecosystem services are the vital benefits that natural systems provide to support human life, economic activities, and environmental stability.

Importance of water security, carbon sequestration, and pollination

Ecosystems provide essential services that sustain life on Earth, including water security, carbon sequestration, and pollination. These interconnected services play a critical role in supporting human wellbeing, economic activities, and environmental resilience.

Water Security

Water security is vital for sustaining life, agriculture, and industry, and ecosystems are key to maintaining reliable and clean water supplies. Forests, wetlands, and watersheds act as natural water filters, removing pollutants and regulating water flow. Wetlands store excess water during floods and release it during dry periods, ensuring a steady supply of freshwater. Forested watersheds help maintain water quality by preventing soil erosion and reducing sediment runoff into rivers and lakes.

Human activities that degrade these ecosystems, such as deforestation and pollution, threaten water security by reducing the availability of clean water. Protecting and restoring natural ecosystems is essential for ensuring water access and resilience to climate impacts, such as droughts and floods.

Carbon Sequestration

Carbon sequestration is a critical ecosystem service in mitigating climate change. Forests, grasslands, and oceans absorb and store significant amounts of carbon dioxide from the atmosphere, reducing greenhouse gas concentrations and slowing global warming. For example, mangroves and peatlands are highly efficient carbon sinks, storing more carbon per unit area than many terrestrial ecosystems.

Deforestation and land degradation release stored carbon, exacerbating climate change. Restoring degraded ecosystems and protecting carbon-rich environments like tropical forests and wetlands are vital strategies for enhancing global carbon sequestration and achieving climate goals.

Pollination

Pollination is essential for food production and biodiversity. Pollinators, such as bees, butterflies, birds, and bats, facilitate the reproduction of plants, including many crops that provide fruits, vegetables, nuts, and seeds. Approximately 75% of global food crops depend on pollination, making it a cornerstone of agricultural productivity and food security.

Habitat destruction, pesticide use, and climate change threaten pollinator populations, posing significant risks to food systems and ecosystems. Protecting pollinator habitats, reducing pesticide use, and planting diverse crops can support pollinator health and ensure the continued provision of this invaluable service.

Water security, carbon sequestration, and pollination are indispensable ecosystem services that underpin human survival, economic activities, and environmental health. By conserving and restoring ecosystems that provide these services, we can build resilience to climate change, enhance food security, and ensure sustainable access to vital resources for future generations.

Economic valuation of ecosystem services

Ecosystem services, such as clean water, climate regulation, and biodiversity, provide immense value to human societies and economies. By assigning monetary value to these services, economic valuation helps highlight their importance, guide policy decisions, and encourage investments in conservation and restoration.

Types of Ecosystem Services

Ecosystem services are commonly categorized into four groups:

1. Provisioning Services: Tangible goods such as food, timber, and fresh water.
2. Regulating Services: Benefits from ecosystem processes, including carbon sequestration, flood control, and water filtration.
3. Cultural Services: Non-material benefits, such as recreational opportunities and spiritual enrichment.
4. Supporting Services: Underlying processes, like nutrient cycling and soil formation, that sustain all other services.

Methods of Economic Valuation

- Market-Based Approaches: Directly valuing ecosystem goods sold in markets, such as fish or timber.
- Replacement Cost Method: Estimating the cost of replacing ecosystem services with man-made alternatives, like building water treatment plants to replace wetlands.

- Willingness to Pay: Assessing how much people are willing to pay for access to ecosystem services, such as national parks.
- Cost of Inaction: Calculating the economic losses from ecosystem degradation, such as reduced agricultural yields due to pollinator loss.

For example, the global value of pollination services is estimated at $235–$577 billion annually, emphasizing the critical role of healthy ecosystems in supporting agriculture and economies.

Economic Benefits of Ecosystem Valuation

Economic valuation creates a compelling argument for conservation by linking ecosystem health to financial gains and cost savings. For instance:

5. Protecting mangroves can save millions annually in flood damage prevention.
6. Restoring wetlands can reduce the need for expensive water filtration infrastructure.
7. Forest conservation reduces greenhouse gas emissions, minimizing costs associated with climate change mitigation.

Valuation also informs sustainable land-use planning by highlighting trade-offs. For example, preserving a forest may yield greater long-term economic benefits through carbon sequestration, tourism, and biodiversity conservation than converting it to agricultural land.

Challenges and Limitations

Valuing ecosystem services is complex, as many benefits are non-market and difficult to quantify. Additionally, focusing solely on monetary value risks overlooking cultural and intrinsic values. Despite these challenges, economic valuation remains a vital tool for integrating nature into decision-making processes.

Economic valuation of ecosystem services underscores their indispensable contributions to human wellbeing and economic stability. By recognizing the true value of ecosystems, governments, businesses, and communities can make informed decisions to conserve and restore natural resources, ensuring long-term sustainability and prosperity.

Conservation Strategies

Conservation strategies provide actionable approaches to protect and restore ecosystems, ensuring the continued provision of essential services and the preservation of biodiversity.

Preserving critical habitats and biodiversity hotspots

Preserving critical habitats and biodiversity hotspots is vital for maintaining global biodiversity, ecosystem services, and the resilience of natural systems. These areas are home to a high concentration of species, many of which are endemic or endangered. Protecting these regions is crucial not only for the survival of the species that inhabit them but also for the broader health of the planet's ecosystems.

What Are Critical Habitats and Biodiversity Hotspots?

Critical habitats are areas essential for the survival of species, often providing key resources like food, shelter, and breeding grounds. These habitats include forests, wetlands, grasslands, mangroves, and coral reefs—ecosystems that support a wide range of biodiversity and perform vital environmental functions, such as carbon sequestration, water purification, and flood regulation.

Biodiversity hotspots, as defined by Conservation International, are regions that are both rich in species and highly threatened by human activities. These areas, although covering just 2.3% of the Earth's land surface, are home to more than 50% of the world's plant species and 43% of bird, mammal, reptile, and amphibian species. The 36 recognized hotspots across the world represent a priority for conservation, as they face significant threats, including deforestation, urbanization, and climate change.

Why Protect These Areas?

- High Concentration of Endemic Species: Hotspots often contain species found nowhere else on Earth, making their preservation crucial for maintaining global biodiversity. For example, the rainforests of the Amazon and the islands of Southeast Asia host a wide variety of endemic species that depend on their unique ecosystems.
- Ecosystem Services: Critical habitats and hotspots provide essential ecosystem services, such as regulating climate, purifying water, controlling flooding, and supporting agriculture through pollination. The loss of these ecosystems leads to a decline in the services that communities rely on for survival and economic stability.
- Global Climate Change Mitigation: Many biodiversity hotspots, such as tropical forests and peatlands, store large amounts of carbon, playing a significant role in global climate regulation. Protecting these areas helps mitigate the effects of climate change by preserving carbon sinks and enhancing climate resilience.
- Economic and Cultural Value: Beyond ecological importance, critical habitats and hotspots contribute to local and global economies through tourism, fisheries, agriculture, and the pharmaceutical industry. They also hold cultural significance for indigenous and local communities who depend on these ecosystems for their livelihoods, traditions, and spiritual practices.

Threats to Critical Habitats and Hotspots

- Deforestation and Land Conversion: One of the greatest threats to critical habitats and biodiversity hotspots is the conversion of land for agriculture, logging, and urban expansion. Forests are cleared to make way for crops like soy and palm oil or for timber production, leading to the loss of habitat for countless species.

- Climate Change: Climate change exacerbates existing threats, altering ecosystems and pushing species out of their natural ranges. Rising temperatures, changing precipitation patterns, and extreme weather events such as droughts, floods, and hurricanes place additional pressure on these fragile ecosystems.
- Pollution: Pollution from industrial and agricultural runoff, plastic waste, and chemicals also threatens biodiversity hotspots, damaging habitats and poisoning species.
- Overexploitation: Unsustainable hunting, fishing, and harvesting of natural resources further depletes the populations of endangered species, pushing them toward extinction.

Conservation Approaches and Strategies

- Protected Areas: Establishing national parks, nature reserves, and marine protected areas is one of the most effective ways to conserve critical habitats. These areas provide legal protection against destructive activities like logging, mining, and fishing, ensuring that ecosystems can thrive without human interference.
- Habitat Restoration: In areas where ecosystems have been degraded, habitat restoration is crucial to rebuild ecological functions. This may involve replanting native species, restoring wetlands, or rehabilitating coral reefs, all of which help improve biodiversity and the resilience of ecosystems.
- Sustainable Land Use: Implementing sustainable land-use practices, such as agroforestry, sustainable agriculture, and eco-friendly tourism, can help reduce the pressure on critical habitats. These practices ensure that human development does not come at the expense of biodiversity.
- Community Engagement and Indigenous Knowledge: Involving local and indigenous communities in conservation

efforts is essential. These communities often have deep knowledge of local ecosystems and sustainable practices that can contribute to habitat preservation. Co-management models, where local people and conservationists work together, have been effective in protecting biodiversity while improving the livelihoods of communities.

Preserving critical habitats and biodiversity hotspots is essential for maintaining the planet's biodiversity, supporting human wellbeing, and ensuring environmental stability. By implementing effective conservation strategies, such as protecting areas, restoring ecosystems, and promoting sustainable practices, we can safeguard these vital regions for future generations, ensuring that the rich diversity of life on Earth continues to thrive.

Sustainable land-use planning

Sustainable land-use planning is a crucial approach for balancing human development with the preservation of natural resources and ecosystem services. As the global population grows and urbanization expands, the demand for land increases, putting immense pressure on ecosystems, biodiversity, and the environment. Sustainable land-use planning seeks to integrate environmental, social, and economic considerations to manage land resources in a way that promotes long-term sustainability, reduces environmental degradation, and enhances the quality of life for current and future generations.

Key Principles of Sustainable Land-Use Planning

- Resource Efficiency: Sustainable land-use planning aims to use land and natural resources in the most efficient manner possible. This involves optimizing land allocation for various uses, including agriculture, forestry, and urban development, while minimizing waste and avoiding over-exploitation.
- Ecological Balance: Protecting natural habitats, biodiversity, and ecosystem services is a fundamental principle of sustainable land-use planning. This requires understanding

and respecting the ecological characteristics of different regions, including the capacity of land to support agricultural production, biodiversity, and other ecosystem functions.

- Integration of Environmental and Socioeconomic Factors: Sustainable land-use planning takes into account the needs and rights of local communities, as well as the environmental impact of land use. It promotes inclusive decision-making and ensures that development activities do not undermine the social and cultural fabric of communities or damage the environment.
- Resilience and Adaptability: Sustainable land-use planning aims to enhance the resilience of landscapes to climate change and other environmental stresses. This involves incorporating flexible and adaptive management strategies that allow for the protection and restoration of ecosystems, even in the face of unpredictable environmental changes.

Approaches to Sustainable Land-Use Planning

- Zoning and Land Allocation: Zoning involves designating land for specific purposes, such as agriculture, urban development, conservation, or recreation. Through zoning, planners can control land-use change, ensuring that development occurs in suitable areas while protecting critical ecosystems. Land allocation policies can prioritize the preservation of sensitive areas, such as wetlands, forests, and biodiversity hotspots, while also allowing for sustainable agricultural and urban expansion.
- Agroforestry and Sustainable Agriculture: Integrating trees and vegetation into agricultural landscapes, known as agroforestry, is an important sustainable land-use strategy. Agroforestry not only helps increase agricultural productivity but also conserves biodiversity, improves soil fertility, and enhances carbon sequestration. Sustainable agriculture, including practices such as crop rotation, organic farming, and water-efficient irrigation, reduces the environmental impact of food production while maintaining long-term soil health.

- Ecosystem-based Land Management: This approach uses natural processes to manage land and conserve biodiversity. It includes activities such as reforestation, wetland restoration, and soil erosion control, which help protect and restore ecosystems that provide vital services like water purification, flood regulation, and carbon storage. Ecosystem-based management seeks to enhance the resilience of landscapes to environmental shocks, such as floods, droughts, and land degradation.
- Urban Planning and Green Infrastructure: As urbanization continues, sustainable land-use planning plays a key role in shaping cities that are environmentally responsible, socially equitable, and economically vibrant. Green infrastructure, such as parks, green roofs, and urban forests, enhances biodiversity, improves air and water quality, and mitigates the effects of urban heat islands. Compact, mixed-use urban development reduces sprawl, promotes energy efficiency, and minimizes transportation emissions.

Challenges in Sustainable Land-Use Planning

- Conflicting Interests: One of the main challenges in sustainable land-use planning is balancing competing interests, such as economic development, agriculture, and conservation. In many cases, land-use decisions are influenced by short-term economic gains, such as increased agricultural output or urban expansion, which may undermine long-term environmental sustainability.
- Political and Institutional Barriers: Effective land-use planning requires coordination across multiple sectors, government agencies, and levels of government. In many cases, institutional fragmentation and a lack of political will hinder the development and implementation of cohesive land-use policies.
- Climate Change and Environmental Degradation: Climate change, habitat loss, and environmental degradation exacerbate the challenges of sustainable land-use planning. Shifting weather patterns, desertification, and biodiversity

loss affect land productivity and necessitate more adaptive and forward-thinking land-use strategies.

Benefits of Sustainable Land-Use Planning

- Enhanced Ecosystem Services: By prioritizing the protection and restoration of ecosystems, sustainable land-use planning enhances the provision of ecosystem services, such as clean water, carbon sequestration, and pollination, which are essential for human wellbeing and economic prosperity.
- Increased Resilience: Sustainable land-use practices help communities adapt to climate change, natural disasters, and other environmental stresses. Restoring wetlands, for example, can reduce flooding risks, while agroforestry systems increase agricultural resilience to droughts and soil erosion.
- Economic Sustainability: Sustainable land-use planning supports long-term economic growth by promoting resource efficiency, reducing environmental costs, and ensuring that natural resources remain available for future generations. By incorporating environmental considerations into land-use policies, businesses can reduce operational risks and increase their resilience to environmental changes.

Sustainable land-use planning is essential for achieving long-term environmental sustainability, economic prosperity, and social equity. By integrating ecological, social, and economic considerations into land management, countries and communities can ensure that development meets the needs of present and future generations while conserving vital natural resources and ecosystem services. Through sustainable land-use practices such as agroforestry, ecosystem-based management, and green infrastructure, we can create resilient, thriving landscapes that support both people and the planet.

Promoting community-based conservation

Community-based conservation (CBC) is an approach that empowers local communities to actively engage in the management and protection of natural resources and ecosystems. This method integrates traditional ecological knowledge with modern conservation strategies, ensuring that conservation efforts are locally driven, culturally appropriate, and sustainable. By involving communities in decision-making, CBC fosters ownership, builds capacity, and helps maintain biodiversity while improving the livelihoods of people who depend on natural resources.

The Role of Local Communities in Conservation

Local communities are often the primary stewards of natural resources, with deep knowledge of their ecosystems gained over generations. Community-based conservation capitalizes on this knowledge, allowing local people to lead conservation efforts and make decisions that reflect their needs and cultural values. Communities are usually more familiar with the land, wildlife, and threats to their environment, making them well-positioned to implement effective, localized conservation actions.

In many regions, local communities are disproportionately affected by environmental degradation, such as deforestation, soil erosion, and water scarcity. When these communities are involved in conservation, they not only help protect the environment but also benefit directly from the sustainable management of resources, such as through eco-tourism, sustainable agriculture, and non-timber forest products.

Key Components of Community-Based Conservation

- Participatory Decision-Making: At the core of CBC is the active involvement of local people in the planning, implementation, and monitoring of conservation initiatives. This participatory approach ensures that conservation strategies align with local needs and priorities, increasing the likelihood of success.
- Capacity Building: Empowering local communities through training and education is vital for the sustainability of CBC.

Skills in sustainable land management, natural resource conservation, and eco-tourism provide local people with tools to manage their environments and create sustainable livelihoods.

- Collaboration with External Stakeholders: Successful CBC often involves partnerships between local communities, governments, NGOs, and private sector actors. These collaborations bring together resources, expertise, and funding, helping to scale up conservation efforts while maintaining local control.
- Cultural and Traditional Knowledge: Indigenous and local knowledge systems play a crucial role in conservation. Many communities have long-standing traditions of resource management, such as rotational farming or sacred natural areas, which can be incorporated into modern conservation strategies. Respecting and integrating this knowledge helps ensure that conservation efforts are both culturally appropriate and effective.

Benefits of Community-Based Conservation

- Biodiversity Preservation: Involving local communities in conservation helps protect critical habitats and species. Studies have shown that community-managed protected areas and conservation initiatives often have higher success rates than top-down, externally driven projects.
- Sustainable Livelihoods: CBC provides opportunities for communities to develop sustainable livelihoods. Eco-tourism, sustainable harvesting of non-timber forest products (such as medicinal plants or honey), and the promotion of organic agriculture can generate income while ensuring that natural resources are preserved for future generations.
- Increased Resilience: Communities engaged in conservation are better equipped to adapt to environmental changes and climate-related challenges. By promoting sustainable land management and resource use, CBC strengthens the resilience of local ecosystems and the communities that depend on them.

- Social Empowerment: CBC empowers communities by recognizing their role in environmental stewardship and decision-making. This approach fosters social cohesion, strengthens local governance, and provides communities with a sense of ownership over their natural heritage.

Challenges to Community-Based Conservation

- Conflicting Interests: Often, there are competing interests between conservation and development goals. For example, local communities may rely on natural resources for their livelihoods, but large-scale agricultural or infrastructure projects may threaten these resources. Balancing these interests requires careful negotiation and compromise.
- Limited Resources: While CBC initiatives can be highly effective, they often require external support in terms of funding, training, and expertise. Ensuring that communities have access to the necessary resources and tools is critical for success.
- Legal and Political Barriers: In some regions, land tenure and resource rights are not clearly defined, making it difficult for communities to assert control over their natural resources. Legal frameworks that support community rights and governance are essential for the success of CBC.

Successful Examples of Community-Based Conservation

- The Namibian Communal Conservancy Program: In Namibia, the government has worked with local communities to establish conservancies that manage wildlife and natural resources. This model has been successful in both conserving biodiversity and providing economic benefits through sustainable tourism and hunting.
- The Maasai Mara in Kenya: The Maasai Mara region, home to the Maasai people, has seen successful community-led conservation initiatives focused on protecting wildlife corridors and reducing human-wildlife conflict. Community-

based approaches have helped maintain a balance between conservation and the traditional livelihoods of the Maasai.

Promoting community-based conservation is an effective strategy for ensuring the long-term health of ecosystems and the wellbeing of local communities. By integrating local knowledge, fostering collaboration, and empowering communities, CBC creates sustainable solutions that benefit both people and the environment. This approach is crucial for the conservation of biodiversity, the preservation of ecosystem services, and the promotion of social equity in a rapidly changing world.

Financing Ecosystem Restoration

Financing ecosystem restoration is essential for scaling up efforts to repair damaged ecosystems, ensuring long-term ecological health, and supporting sustainable development goals.

Carbon credits and ecosystem service payments

Carbon credits and ecosystem service payments (ESPs) are innovative financial mechanisms that incentivize the protection and restoration of ecosystems while promoting sustainable development. These mechanisms link environmental services, such as carbon sequestration and biodiversity conservation, to economic rewards, enabling both public and private sectors to contribute to ecological sustainability.

Carbon Credits

Carbon credits are tradable certificates or permits that represent a unit of carbon dioxide (CO_2) emissions reduced or sequestered. The concept of carbon credits is part of carbon markets, which allow businesses, governments, and other entities to meet their emissions reduction targets through offsetting activities. Each carbon credit typically represents one metric ton of CO_2 that has been avoided, reduced, or removed from the atmosphere through activities such as reforestation, renewable energy projects, and improved land-use practices.

Carbon credit systems are governed by international frameworks, such as the Kyoto Protocol and the Paris Agreement, which set emissions reduction targets for countries. Under these frameworks, projects that reduce or absorb CO_2—such as planting trees in deforested areas or capturing methane from landfills—are awarded carbon credits. These credits can be bought and sold in voluntary or compliance carbon markets, allowing entities that exceed their emissions limits to offset their excess emissions by purchasing credits from carbon-reducing projects.

ESPs

ESPs are financial incentives provided to landowners, communities, or organizations that manage or protect ecosystems that deliver essential services, such as clean water, flood control, pollination, or soil fertility. ESPs are designed to reward those who contribute to the conservation and restoration of ecosystems that provide benefits to society, often in the form of payments for the continued preservation of natural resources.

For example, a government or corporation might pay farmers or landowners to adopt sustainable land management practices, such as agroforestry, that enhance carbon storage, reduce water usage, or preserve biodiversity. Similarly, communities that protect wetlands, mangroves, or forests may receive financial support for their efforts to maintain these critical ecosystems and the services they provide, such as disaster risk reduction or water filtration.

The Role of Carbon Credits and ESPs in Ecosystem Restoration

Both carbon credits and ESPs have emerged as essential tools in financing ecosystem restoration projects. These mechanisms provide a sustainable revenue stream for projects focused on restoring degraded ecosystems, such as reforesting areas affected by logging or reintroducing natural vegetation to improve water retention in dry regions. For example, projects that restore tropical rainforests can generate carbon credits by sequestering CO_2, while simultaneously benefiting local communities through the provision of water and food security, pollination, and flood regulation.

In addition, these financial mechanisms help align the interests of local communities, governments, and businesses with the goals of environmental conservation. By providing a tangible economic incentive for ecosystem services, such as carbon sequestration, clean water, and biodiversity, they help create a shared responsibility for maintaining and restoring vital ecosystems. In this way, carbon credits and ESPs support sustainable land management practices, help prevent further environmental degradation, and contribute to the global efforts to combat climate change.

Challenges and Criticism

While carbon credits and ESPs have the potential to significantly scale up ecosystem restoration efforts, there are challenges and criticisms associated with their implementation. One challenge is ensuring that the carbon credits generated are additional, meaning that the emissions reductions would not have occurred without the specific project. Without clear guidelines and verification systems, there is a risk of "greenwashing," where projects are credited for emissions reductions that may not be real or permanent.

In the case of ESPs, concerns include the equitable distribution of payments and the effectiveness of payments in incentivizing long-term conservation. In some cases, ESPs may not be sufficient to motivate landowners or communities to maintain ecosystem services, particularly when they face competing pressures to exploit land for agriculture or development. Furthermore, there is a need for better integration of these mechanisms into broader land-use and development policies to ensure that they contribute to sustainable outcomes.

Future Prospects

Despite these challenges, the future of carbon credits and ESPs looks promising. The growing recognition of the value of ecosystem services, coupled with the urgency of addressing climate change and biodiversity loss, is driving further innovation and investment in these mechanisms. In particular, increasing corporate involvement and demand for carbon credits is helping to expand markets and incentivize larger-scale restoration projects. Additionally, there are efforts to improve the transparency, monitoring, and verification systems for both carbon credits and ESPs, ensuring that the benefits of these mechanisms are real, measurable, and lasting.

Carbon credits and ESPs are integral to the future of ecosystem restoration, providing essential funding and incentives for the protection and restoration of natural systems. By aligning environmental goals with economic incentives, these mechanisms help ensure the sustainability of ecosystem services, mitigate climate change, and support local livelihoods. To fully realize their potential, ongoing efforts to improve transparency, accountability, and equity are necessary to ensure that these financial tools contribute effectively to a Nature Positive Economy.

Debt-for-nature swaps and philanthropic funding

Debt-for-nature swaps and philanthropic funding are innovative financial mechanisms designed to support environmental conservation and sustainable development. These approaches help address the significant funding gaps in conservation efforts, providing financial resources to protect ecosystems and biodiversity while relieving economic burdens on countries facing high levels of debt. Both strategies offer creative ways to mobilize private capital for environmental causes and integrate financial solutions with conservation objectives.

Debt-for-Nature Swaps

Debt-for-nature swaps are agreements where a portion of a country's external debt is forgiven in exchange for the country committing to invest in environmental conservation efforts. The arrangement is typically facilitated by international organizations, conservation NGOs, and government institutions. The primary goal of these swaps is to reduce the financial pressure on countries while ensuring that the funds freed up are used for ecological restoration, biodiversity protection, or sustainable resource management.

Debt-for-nature swaps began in the 1980s and were initially applied to countries with significant national debts and vulnerable ecosystems, particularly in Latin America. Under these agreements, the government of a debt-stricken country commits to allocate funds that would otherwise go toward debt repayment for conservation projects. In return, the creditors agree to cancel part or all of the country's outstanding debt.

For example, in 1998, the United States and several international donors, including the World Bank and conservation groups, facilitated a debt-for-nature swap for Costa Rica, resulting in the cancellation of $26 million of Costa Rica's national debt. In exchange, Costa Rica allocated funds toward the preservation of its tropical forests and biodiversity. Such swaps have proven successful in both reducing debt and enhancing environmental protection, ensuring that the economic benefits of debt relief go hand-in-hand with ecosystem restoration.

Benefits of Debt-for-Nature Swaps

- Debt Relief: Countries with high levels of debt can use the money freed by the cancellation of debt to support environmental programs instead of servicing international loans.
- Conservation Financing: These swaps provide crucial funding for biodiversity conservation, ecosystem restoration, and sustainable development, helping countries protect their natural heritage.

- Strengthened International Cooperation: Debt-for-nature swaps foster international collaboration, as these initiatives often involve a range of stakeholders, including governments, international financial institutions, and conservation organizations.
- Enhanced Sustainability: Debt-for-nature swaps are designed to ensure that long-term conservation strategies are funded, making them a sustainable solution for countries looking to balance environmental conservation with economic development.

Challenges of Debt-for-Nature Swaps

Despite their successes, debt-for-nature swaps have limitations. One significant challenge is that the amount of debt forgiven may not always match the scale of the environmental goals. Additionally, the political stability and governance capacity of the debtor country are essential for ensuring that the funds are used effectively for conservation. Some critics argue that these swaps may not always lead to meaningful or long-term environmental benefits without strong monitoring and transparent governance mechanisms.

Philanthropic Funding

Philanthropic funding, provided by private donors, foundations, and CSR initiatives, is another key source of financial support for conservation and environmental projects. Philanthropy plays a crucial role in funding initiatives that governments and businesses might not prioritize or be able to support due to financial constraints. Foundations such as the Bill and Melinda Gates Foundation, Ford Foundation, and Rockefeller Foundation have been instrumental in supporting initiatives that align with their mission to address climate change, protect biodiversity, and ensure sustainable development.

Philanthropic funding can support a wide range of activities, including:

- On-the-Ground Conservation Projects: Local and community-based conservation efforts can receive direct funding, including wildlife protection, habitat restoration, and environmental education.
- Research and Innovation: Foundations often fund research initiatives focused on developing new conservation technologies, improving agricultural practices, or exploring sustainable solutions to climate change.
- Advocacy and Policy Development: Philanthropic organizations can also contribute to shaping policy and advocacy efforts aimed at strengthening environmental laws and regulations at local, national, and global levels.

Benefits of Philanthropic Funding

- Flexibility: Philanthropic funding is often more flexible and less bureaucratic than government or multilateral financial assistance. This allows for quick mobilization and support of innovative and pilot programs.
- Global Reach: Large foundations have the resources and networks to fund projects on a global scale, targeting priority conservation areas, such as tropical rainforests, coral reefs, and protected marine areas.
- Long-Term Impact: Many philanthropic organizations are committed to long-term environmental goals and often provide multi-year funding commitments that help build sustainable conservation projects.

Challenges of Philanthropic Funding

- Dependence on Private Sources: Over-reliance on philanthropy can lead to uneven funding and project stability, especially if funding priorities shift or philanthropic resources are stretched thin.
- Accountability and Transparency: Like debt-for-nature swaps, philanthropic funding requires careful oversight to ensure that it is used effectively and equitably, especially in remote or politically unstable regions.

Both debt-for-nature swaps and philanthropic funding are valuable tools for financing ecosystem restoration and conservation projects. They provide essential resources for countries and communities struggling with financial challenges while helping to protect critical ecosystems and biodiversity. While there are challenges in implementation and sustainability, these financial mechanisms offer creative ways to support environmental goals and foster long-term, collaborative conservation efforts. By combining innovative financial solutions with strong governance and local engagement, debt-for-nature swaps and philanthropic funding contribute to building a NPE that prioritizes ecological restoration and sustainable development.

Collaborative Models for Success

Collaborative models for success bring together diverse stakeholders, including governments, businesses, and communities, to work towards shared environmental goals and sustainable outcomes.

Role of multi-stakeholder partnerships

Multi-stakeholder partnerships play a critical role in achieving sustainable development and conservation goals by bringing together a diverse range of actors, including governments, businesses, NGOs, local communities, and international institutions. These partnerships enable the pooling of resources, expertise, and knowledge to address complex environmental challenges that require collective action and long-term collaboration.

Collaboration for Shared Goals

One of the key strengths of multi-stakeholder partnerships is their ability to align the interests of various sectors toward common environmental and social objectives. For example, governments can provide regulatory frameworks and policy support, while businesses contribute investment and innovative technologies. NGOs and local communities often bring crucial on-the-ground knowledge and expertise in conservation and sustainable practices. This collaborative approach ensures that all perspectives are considered, leading to more comprehensive and effective solutions.

Leveraging Resources and Expertise

Multi-stakeholder partnerships allow for resource-sharing, which is essential for tackling large-scale environmental issues such as climate change, biodiversity loss, and deforestation. By combining financial resources, technical knowledge, and human capital, these partnerships can mobilize efforts that would be difficult for any one actor to achieve alone. Businesses, for instance, can provide funding for research and development, while NGOs can guide the implementation of conservation strategies, ensuring that solutions are both scientifically sound and culturally appropriate.

Scaling Impact and Building Resilience

Multi-stakeholder partnerships are particularly effective at scaling conservation and sustainability initiatives. By working together, partners can implement projects on a larger scale and create systemic change that influences broader regional or global efforts. These partnerships also build resilience by diversifying inputs and enhancing the capacity of communities and stakeholders to respond to changing environmental conditions.

Multi-stakeholder partnerships are essential for tackling the complex challenges of environmental conservation and sustainable development. Through collaboration, resource-sharing, and leveraging diverse expertise, these partnerships help create scalable, inclusive solutions that drive positive change for both people and the planet.

Examples of successful collaborations

Successful collaborations between governments, businesses, NGOs, and local communities have led to significant advancements in environmental conservation and sustainable development. These partnerships demonstrate the power of collective action in addressing global challenges.

The Amazon Cooperation Treaty Organization (ACTO)

ACTO is a collaboration between eight countries in the Amazon Basin focused on the conservation of the Amazon rainforest. The organization works to promote sustainable development, reduce deforestation, and protect biodiversity in one of the world's most critical ecosystems. Through coordinated policies and joint conservation efforts, ACTO has achieved significant strides in reducing illegal logging and enhancing community-based conservation programs.

The Great Green Wall Initiative

The African Union, governments, NGOs, and local communities are collaborating to combat desertification and land degradation in the Sahel region of Africa. The Great Green Wall aims to restore 100 million hectares of land by planting trees, rehabilitating degraded lands, and improving local livelihoods. This initiative has brought together various stakeholders to combat climate change, enhance food security, and provide sustainable employment opportunities.

The Coral Triangle Initiative

This collaboration involves six countries in the Asia-Pacific region, focused on protecting marine biodiversity, especially coral reefs. Governments, NGOs, and local communities work together to establish marine protected areas, regulate fisheries, and promote sustainable tourism. The initiative has successfully protected marine ecosystems, enhanced local economies, and improved resilience to climate change.

Conclusion

In conclusion, the path to a NPE requires collective action, commitment, and innovation from all sectors of society.

Key Themes Recap: Overview of the Nature Positive Economy Framework and Strategies

The NPE framework represents a transformative approach to sustainable development that places environmental health and human wellbeing at its core. It seeks to create an economic model that not only conserves and restores natural ecosystems but also ensures that economic growth, social development, and environmental sustainability are intertwined. This approach offers a comprehensive strategy for integrating biodiversity conservation, ecosystem restoration, and resource management into the fabric of economic systems, industries, and policies.

Core Principles of the Nature Positive Economy

At the heart of the NPE framework are the principles of environmental health, equity, and resilience. The focus is on ensuring that nature's contributions to human wellbeing, such as clean air, water, food security, and climate regulation, are preserved and enhanced. A NPE goes beyond simply reducing harm to nature—it aims to restore ecosystems, reverse biodiversity loss, and promote sustainable practices across industries.

The NPE framework also emphasizes inclusivity, recognizing that the people most impacted by environmental degradation are often the most vulnerable. This involves creating opportunities for local communities, especially indigenous populations, to engage in decision-making processes and benefit from sustainable economic practices. Ensuring the equitable distribution of benefits is fundamental to achieving social and environmental justice.

Key Strategies for Achieving a Nature Positive Economy

Some key strategies for achieving a NPE include:

- Protection and Restoration of Ecosystems: Central to the NPE framework is the need to protect critical ecosystems and biodiversity hotspots. This includes forests, wetlands, coral reefs, and grasslands, which provide essential services such as carbon sequestration, water filtration, and climate regulation. Strategies involve creating protected areas, implementing habitat restoration projects, and addressing threats such as pollution, over-exploitation, and land conversion.
- Integration of NbS: Nature-based solutions are an innovative approach that uses natural processes to address societal challenges. These include initiatives like reforestation, coastal restoration, and the creation of green infrastructure in urban areas. By integrating NbS into sectors such as agriculture, urban planning, and water management, businesses and governments can enhance climate resilience, reduce environmental degradation, and create sustainable economic opportunities.
- Sustainable Land and Resource Management: The NPE framework advocates for the adoption of sustainable land-use practices, such as agroforestry, sustainable agriculture, and responsible forestry management. By ensuring that land and resources are used in ways that enhance ecosystem services, rather than depleting them, industries and communities can benefit from long-term resource availability and biodiversity conservation.
- Circular Economy Approaches: The circular economy plays a crucial role in a NPE by reducing waste, promoting recycling, and minimizing the extraction of natural resources. By designing products for durability, repairability, and recyclability, industries can reduce their environmental footprint, lower carbon emissions, and create new business models that contribute to sustainability.

- Green Innovation and Technology: Innovations in green technologies, such as renewable energy, energy efficiency, and sustainable materials, are integral to the transition to a Nature Positive Economy. These technologies can help decouple economic growth from environmental harm, enabling industries to reduce emissions, enhance resource efficiency, and adopt cleaner production processes.

- Policy and Regulatory Frameworks: Governments play a critical role in the success of the NPE by implementing policies and regulations that incentivize sustainable practices and hold industries accountable. This includes carbon pricing, biodiversity conservation laws, subsidies for green technologies, and regulations to curb pollution. The role of international agreements and frameworks, such as the Paris Agreement on climate change and the UN Convention on Biological Diversity, also strengthens global cooperation toward a Nature Positive Economy.
- Inclusive Financing Models: Financing is one of the most significant challenges for achieving a Nature Positive Economy. Sustainable investment models, including green bonds, impact investing, and debt-for-nature swaps, provide critical funding for environmental projects. These financial mechanisms incentivize businesses, governments, and communities to invest in conservation and restoration efforts while also ensuring long-term financial returns. The integration of biodiversity and ecosystem service valuation into financial systems further aligns capital flows with environmental goals.

Overall, the NPE framework offers a roadmap for a sustainable, resilient, and inclusive future. By focusing on the restoration of ecosystems, the adoption of nature-based solutions, and the integration of sustainability into all sectors, the NPE represents an economic model that balances the needs of people and the planet. Key strategies include ecosystem protection, sustainable resource management, green innovation, and inclusive financing. Through collaboration among governments, businesses, and communities, the

NPE has the potential to foster a future where environmental health and human prosperity go hand in hand.

Call to Action

Encouragement for Businesses, Governments, and Communities to Act

The transition to a NPE is not a choice but a necessity for ensuring a sustainable and resilient future for both people and the planet. The urgency of addressing the intertwined crises of biodiversity loss, climate change, and ecosystem degradation demands immediate and concerted action from businesses, governments, and communities alike. Each of these sectors plays a unique and vital role in driving the transformation toward a Nature Positive future, and it is only through collaborative efforts that we can achieve meaningful change.

Businesses are critical drivers of economic activity and environmental impact, making their role in the transition to a NPE indispensable. By adopting sustainable practices, businesses can reduce their environmental footprint, create new economic opportunities, and ensure long-term profitability. Companies that integrate sustainability into their core operations benefit from increased resilience, improved risk management, and access to new markets and consumer segments that prioritize environmentally responsible products and services.

However, businesses must go beyond CSR programs. They must embed sustainability into their business models, product designs, and supply chains. Whether through embracing circular economy principles, investing in renewable energy, or adopting nature-based solutions, businesses must act as stewards of both the environment and their communities. The private sector has the resources, innovation, and influence to drive large-scale change, and by committing to sustainability, businesses can contribute to global climate and biodiversity goals while benefiting from the economic opportunities that come with being at the forefront of environmental responsibility.

Governments have a critical responsibility in setting the framework for sustainable development and ensuring that environmental policies are implemented effectively. Through strong regulatory frameworks, financial incentives, and international cooperation, governments can create the conditions that foster the growth of a Nature Positive Economy. This includes implementing policies that encourage sustainable land use, protect natural resources, and hold industries accountable for their environmental impacts.

Governments must invest in the restoration of ecosystems, support the development of green infrastructure, and promote the adoption of nature-based solutions across sectors. Incentives such as subsidies for renewable energy, green infrastructure development, and eco-friendly technologies will help businesses and communities transition to more sustainable practices. Additionally, governments should prioritize policies that integrate biodiversity protection into their development plans and make biodiversity loss and climate change central to their policy agendas.

Moreover, governments have the power to catalyze international collaboration, ensuring that environmental challenges are addressed on a global scale. By leading international agreements on climate change, biodiversity conservation, and sustainable development, governments can create the collective action needed to achieve a Nature Positive Economy.

Communities, particularly local and indigenous populations, are at the heart of conservation and restoration efforts. Their traditional knowledge, stewardship practices, and deep connections to the land make them indispensable allies in the global effort to protect ecosystems and biodiversity. Community-based conservation initiatives, such as sustainable land management, agroforestry, and indigenous-led conservation practices, offer powerful solutions to the environmental challenges we face today.

However, communities also need support from both governments and businesses. Ensuring that local populations have the resources, knowledge, and capacity to engage in sustainable practices is essential. This means providing financial resources, training, and access to markets for eco-friendly products and services. Equally important is empowering communities to take leadership roles in decision-making processes related to natural resource management, ensuring that their voices are heard and that their rights to land and resources are protected.

Communities also play a crucial role in raising awareness and driving grassroots efforts for environmental change. By fostering a culture of sustainability, communities can influence broader social and political change, pushing for stronger environmental protections and more sustainable development practices at the local, national, and global levels.

The challenges we face—biodiversity loss, climate change, and ecosystem degradation—are urgent and require immediate action. Delay in addressing these issues will lead to irreversible damage to ecosystems, economies, and communities worldwide. However, the opportunity to transition to a NPE is still within reach. By acting now, businesses, governments, and communities can set the foundation for a resilient, prosperous future that benefits all.

For businesses, the time to act is now. By making sustainability a core part of their operations, they can reduce risk, unlock new markets, and ensure their long-term viability. Governments must seize this moment to implement policies that incentivize sustainable development and hold industries accountable for their environmental impact. Communities must continue to advocate for their rights, engage in sustainable practices, and support local conservation efforts.

The transition to a NPE requires a collective, global effort. Businesses, governments, and communities must all take responsibility for the environment and work together to ensure a sustainable future for generations to come. Through collaboration, innovation, and commitment, we can achieve a world where economic prosperity and environmental health go hand in hand. The time to act is now, and every sector has an essential role to play in making a NPE a reality.

Practical Steps for Individuals to Contribute

While large-scale systemic changes are crucial for achieving a Nature Positive Economy, individuals also play an essential role in driving sustainability and environmental protection. By making informed choices and adopting eco-friendly practices in daily life, individuals can contribute significantly to the preservation of ecosystems, biodiversity, and the fight against climate change. The following practical steps highlight how individuals can contribute to a more sustainable and Nature Positive world.

Reduce, Reuse, and Recycle

One of the most effective ways individuals can contribute to sustainability is by reducing their consumption of single-use items, reusing products whenever possible, and recycling materials. By minimizing waste, individuals help reduce the demand for new resources and lower the amount of waste that ends up in landfills or the environment. For example, using reusable bags, bottles, and containers significantly reduces plastic waste, while recycling paper, glass, and metal helps conserve raw materials.

Additionally, purchasing products with minimal packaging, choosing durable items that can be repaired or reused, and avoiding products with harmful chemicals can reduce the environmental footprint of household consumption. Individuals can also compost organic waste to return nutrients to the soil and reduce methane emissions from landfills.

Support Sustainable and Local Agriculture

Individuals can make a significant impact by choosing to support sustainable farming practices. By purchasing locally grown, organic, and sustainably sourced food, individuals help reduce the environmental costs associated with industrial agriculture, such as water pollution, soil degradation, and greenhouse gas emissions from transportation.

Supporting sustainable agricultural practices such as regenerative farming, agroforestry, and permaculture can also help restore ecosystems and promote biodiversity. Furthermore, reducing food waste by planning meals, storing food properly, and consuming leftovers ensures that less food is wasted, which is an important part of reducing the carbon footprint of food production.

Adopt a Sustainable Energy Lifestyle

Reducing energy consumption is a powerful way individuals can contribute to sustainability. Simple steps such as switching to energy-efficient light bulbs, unplugging electronics when not in use, and using appliances with high energy ratings can help lower electricity demand. Additionally, individuals can reduce their reliance on fossil fuels by using public transportation, carpooling, biking, or walking, all of which reduce emissions from vehicles.

For those who have the opportunity, investing in renewable energy sources, such as solar panels for homes, can further reduce one's environmental footprint. Additionally, individuals can reduce their carbon footprint by opting for energy-efficient heating and cooling systems and reducing water heating energy use.

Make Conscious Consumption Choices

Conscious consumption involves making decisions that prioritize sustainability in the products we buy and the companies we support. Individuals can seek out brands and businesses that prioritize sustainability, ethical labor practices, and environmental responsibility. This includes choosing products made from renewable, biodegradable, or recycled materials and those certified by reputable environmental certifications, such as Fair Trade, Rainforest Alliance, or Forest Stewardship Council (FSC).

Moreover, individuals can reduce their environmental impact by buying less, focusing on quality rather than quantity. Avoiding fast fashion by choosing durable clothing made from sustainable materials, or second-hand shopping, can also reduce the demand for resource-intensive production processes.

Advocate for Environmental Protection

Advocacy is a powerful tool for driving policy change, and individuals can use their voices to influence environmental policies at local, national, and global levels. Writing to elected representatives, participating in environmental campaigns, and supporting policies that promote conservation, renewable energy, and pollution reduction can help shift public and political priorities toward sustainability.

Additionally, individuals can join or support environmental organizations and movements that focus on issues such as climate change, deforestation, or biodiversity conservation. By becoming active in these causes, individuals can help amplify their impact through collective action and foster awareness of the importance of preserving ecosystems for future generations.

Educate and Inspire Others

Environmental change starts with awareness, and individuals can contribute by educating themselves and others about the importance of protecting the environment. Sharing knowledge, whether through conversations, social media platforms, or community engagement, can inspire others to adopt sustainable practices. Hosting workshops, participating in clean-up drives, or volunteering for local environmental organizations can also directly contribute to conservation efforts.

Furthermore, leading by example can be a powerful motivator for others to make similar changes in their own lives. Whether it's adopting sustainable practices at home or at work, individuals can demonstrate that living sustainably is not only possible but rewarding.

Support Conservation and Restoration Efforts

Supporting conservation projects—whether through donations, volunteering, or participating in local conservation efforts—can directly contribute to preserving biodiversity and ecosystems. Many organizations and initiatives focus on protecting endangered species, restoring degraded habitats, and combating deforestation. By contributing to these efforts, individuals can help protect vital ecosystems and promote nature-based solutions that benefit both the environment and communities.

Vision for the Future

Imagine a world where nature thrives alongside human progress, where cities are built to harmonize with the environment, and the air we breathe, the water we drink, and the soil beneath our feet are all clean and abundant. In this sustainable, nature-positive world, ecosystems are restored, and biodiversity flourishes, creating a balanced relationship between humanity and the natural world.

In this vision, forests once again blanket vast areas of land, wetlands purify water, and coral reefs teem with life, supporting both marine biodiversity and coastal communities. Agriculture has evolved into a regenerative practice, enriching soils, enhancing food security, and supporting thriving local economies. Green infrastructure in cities provides places for people to connect with nature, while also reducing carbon emissions, managing stormwater, and supporting urban biodiversity.

Governments, businesses, and communities work in unison, guided by a shared commitment to sustainability. Industries have embraced circular economy principles, reducing waste and reusing resources, while adopting renewable energy and responsible production practices. Policies promote conservation, sustainable resource use, and equitable access to nature's benefits, ensuring that no one is left behind in the pursuit of a sustainable future.

In this nature-positive world, communities thrive by drawing on the wisdom of traditional knowledge and modern innovation, and the power of collective action. We live in harmony with the planet, ensuring that future generations inherit a world full of vibrant ecosystems, abundant natural resources, and a sustainable future where both people and nature can prosper together.